John Austin Stevens

Resumption of Specie Payment

A Series of Letters to the New-York Daily Times

John Austin Stevens

Resumption of Specie Payment
A Series of Letters to the New-York Daily Times

ISBN/EAN: 9783744720212

Printed in Europe, USA, Canada, Australia, Japan

Cover: Foto ©Suzi / pixelio.de

More available books at **www.hansebooks.com**

RESUMPTION OF SPECIE PAYMENT.

A SERIES OF LETTERS

TO

The New-York Daily Times,

BY

KNICKERBOCKER.

SEPTEMBER—OCTOBER, 1873.

FOR SALE AT THE OFFICE OF THE NEW-YORK DAILY TIMES, AT BRENTANO'S
LITERARY EMPORIUM, UNION SQUARE, AND BY THE
AMERICAN NEWS COMPANY.

New-York:

JOHN W. AMERMAN, PRINTER,

No. 47 CEDAR STREET.

—

1873.

NOTE.

KNICKERBOCKER, in compliance with a very general request, prints his recent letters to the New-York Times in a pamphlet form. As they were in the outset only intended to invite public attention, through the Press, to what seems to be a simple and practical way of resumption, the constant repetition of the idea, which is the base of the whole argument, was unavoidable. That idea is, that a gradual resumption can be reached by withdrawing paper and substituting coin for the paper withdrawn in the circulating medium, without inflation or contraction.

KNICKERBOCKER owns receipt of a large number of letters and pamphlets, on the subject of American Finance, and tenders to their authors his hearty thanks. He also offers his acknowledgments to the Press throughout the country for its kind notice and general reprint of his Letters.

TABLE OF CONTENTS.

Letter No. I.

OUR OPPORTUNITY.

To the Editor of the New-York Times :

THE eyes of the country are turned upon the Secretary. The occasion is one of those which demand the exercise of the greatest qualities of the mind—firmness, courage and fertility of resource. In such emergencies real power asserts itself, and history accords to the successful minister the highest niche in the temple of fame. Not to HAMILTON, who organized, nor to GALLATIN, whose comprehensive and economic mind developed the administration of the Treasury Department, nor yet to CHASE, who, in the midst of a great war, successfully transformed the cumbrous and irresponsible State bank system to a general banking law, with a homogeneous currency, was such an opportunity afforded as now offers itself to the Secretary of the Treasury.

Though a *debtor nation,* in that our national and corporate obligations are largely held by other nations, while, on the other hand, we hold few, if any, foreign securities, we are a *creditor trade.* The turn of exchanges is in our favor, and must remain so for a considerable period. The crops of both England and France are notoriously deficient, while those of the United States are unusually large. A heavy demand will soon set in from Europe for American breadstuffs, and gold must inevitably flow to this country in payment. Indeed, the stream has already commenced. Last week a million of dollars was received, and to-day's advices report the shipment of another million to New-York and half a million to Canada. The Bank of England sounds the alarm-bell in a first raise of the rate of interest—a warning to the mercantile community of Great Britain to take in sail and prepare for heavy weather.

On the other hand, it is certain that no advance in rate can prevent the shipment of coin in considerable sum to this side. It cannot be doubted that during the last ten days the outstanding orders for purchase of foreign goods for American account have been largely

2

curtailed, (fifty per cent. is a low estimate,) while no new orders are likely to be given in the present condition of affairs.

Very little demand for foreign exchange need be looked for from, or on account of, our importers. How, then, can the exports of grain be paid for by foreign nations, unless by coin or a return of American securities? But experience has shown that our Government securities are just about the last things which the British people, or European nations generally, care to part with. The wise policy of the Government in reducing the extent of the debt has secured a firm holding of it. As for rail-road securities, the tone of the American market is not favorable to that style of remittance just now. It seems inevitable, then, that a more considerable flow of gold than has ever before taken place has already commenced toward this country. The balance of trade is in our favor, and will so remain if the Secretary of the Treasury be equal to the occasion.

In the light of recent experience it may safely be affirmed that the country has " grown up," as the favorite phrase is, to the present volume of the circulating medium, say seven hundred millions dollars greenbacks and national currency. In 1860 the circulating medium was estimated to amount to four hundred and fifty millions, of which two hundred millions were in bank notes and two hundred and fifty millions in gold and silver. In 1860, with gold at par, the sum of national transactions demanded a circulation of four hundred and fifty millions of dollars. In 1873 it demands seven hundred millions, at least it so appears. When the precise measure of the national transactions is reached, and the balance of trade being in our favor there is no export demand for specie, gold should be at par.

What is the price of gold to-day? Had the Secretary not withdrawn from market the amount advertised for sale, this question could have been yesterday answered. Who can answer it to-day? Is it 112, the price nominally fixed by the Gold Board for settlement? This is to assume that in the terrible revulsion of last week, when all other values have been affected—except Government values, sustained by their conversion into currency—gold has neither increased nor diminished in value; that its purchasing power is neither greater nor less than it was ten days since. This is simply absurd. Is it worth more or less? Evidently less, since London exchange is offering freely, without many takers, at 104 per cent.; a nominal premium of 4 per cent., in reality at 4 per cent. discount, the par of exchange being 108 per cent. This would indicate that gold to-day is worth 4 per cent. less than its nominal price, i. e., 108 per cent. If we judge it by currency, which yesterday sold at 3 per cent. premium, then 109 per cent. would appear as its present value. If we judge it by the decline in all other values, it seems more probable that it is worth little, if any thing, above par. We entertain little doubt that if even a moderate sum, say $5,000,000, were added to the gold now on the market, its price would rapidly fall, until those persons who now hoard currency at a premium would exchange their hoard for gold; in other words, until there should be an equalization between gold and greenbacks. This is practical resumption, and every dollar of gold in the country would flow into circulation so soon as this par were reached, while the flow from abroad would weekly add to the amount thus restored to general use. Currency could then be gradually retired, and gold would flow in to fill its place. So long as the exchanges remain favorable, nothing will be necessary to restore specie payment beyond this gradual withdrawal of currency and inflow of gold. The Secretary could, moreover, by direct purchase of gold in foreign markets, contribute in times of necessity to the maintenance of the par of greenbacks.

Let the Secretary continue the sales of gold; let him put upon the market some part of the large sum now held and ascertain its value. A few millions would decide this point beyond a question. If it be not materially above par, as we believe, the step to practical resumption is a slight and easy one. Then out of the "nettle danger we would pluck the flower safety," and the country would find its profit even in the very depth of this calamity. On the other hand, if this occasion be neglected, all thought of resumption of specie payment may as well be abandoned for the next decade at least.

If the policy of the Treasury Department be not shaped toward resumption when the exchanges are in our favor and coin flowing in upon us, we may as well abandon all hope of specie payment in our generation.

I am, sir, yours truly,

KNICKERBOCKER.

NEW-YORK, *September* 27, 1873.

Letter No. II.

OUR TRUE POLICY.

AT every turn the question is now heard, " Are we about to resume specie payment?" The public conscience seems to have at
last accepted the idea of resumption as a sensible idea—as a practical idea—as no longer theoretical and impracticable. What is
practical resumption? The equalization of currency and coin—in
other words, *gold at par.* It lies in the power of the Secretary to
hasten or retard this equalization. The public mind is set against
any undue interference on the part of the Secretary in the financial
affairs of the country. It holds it to be a dangerous thing to
habituate the banking and mercantile classes to such interference.
But there are many ways of interference. Negative action is at
times as effective as positive action. Of this there was a plain
instance during the past week. The sale of gold advertised by the
Secretary was countermanded. This was accepted at once by the
gold speculators as an announcement that the current policy of the
Government was now changed, and that it would no longer put
upon the market its surplus reserve. Rumors were spread of the
weakness of the Treasury. Hence the flurry which carried up the
nominal price of gold to 115⅝, from which it again receded to 112.
We say nominal price, because it is well known that there is not
enough cash gold on the market to afford room for any considerable
transactions—*i. e.,* sale and delivery—and thus to make a real price.
The whole movement was a domestic transaction among the gold
brokers themselves, in which the outside public had little or no
interest.

We ask again, what is the true value of gold? and we repeat in
the words of Saturday, that it can only be ascertained practically
by the sale of say five millions. As there is no demand for export,
and the advices from Great Britain are of continued and increasing
shipments, it is absolutely impossible that there should be any demand for speculative purposes. Who is to buy gold with hope of
profit in the face of large importations? What hinders the Secretary from continuing his sales? It cannot be said that he fears to
deplete the Treasury. A fall in gold would increase rather than

diminish his store, by just so much as such fall would tempt the importer to withdraw his bonded stock from warehouse, and pay his duties into the Treasury. It cannot be that it is because he fears to withdraw currency from the street, because a simultaneous purchase of bonds would immediately restore that currency. What would be the effect of the sale of five millions of gold? We again repeat that gold would fall at once to its real value. So soon as it reached 104 or 103, the price at which currency sold last week, it would be taken by the savings banks for permanent holding, and by the large number of persons who now hoard currency. By exactly the amount of these purchases, currency would be set free to perform its usual offices, to the great relief of the whole community. The gold would not pass into the hands of speculators, for they have no money wherewith to purchase it, even if so inclined, and credit is not money in this time of shrinkage. On the contrary, the gold thus released from the Treasury would pass into the hands of the banking institutions of the country, and there await the near day of resumption. A fall in gold would then be inaugurated, and in a very short time par would probably be reached. When there is more gold offering than there is demand for, as a commodity, it will fall to par, and being useless otherwise, there being neither profit nor hope of profit in keeping it, it will float in the currency. Then the hour will have arrived for the Secretary to take in his greenbacks, while gold, freed from its confinement, will flow in to fill the vacuum thus created. A firm policy on the part of the Government, checking expansion and holding the banks firmly to their engagements, will enable the Secretary, in a period of time, which cannot be measured, and which should not be unduly hastened, to retire the whole of the greenback issue. The circulating medium of the country would then consist of $350,000,000 of coin and of the national bank currency, about the amount the transactions of the country are generally supposed to require, with prices at gold values—that is, with gold at par.

Can there be a more favorable moment for the inauguration of a new policy? The exchanges are in our favor. The gold and silver product of the country will remain with us, and our great crops can only be taken by direct shipment of coin from abroad. The country should resolutely set its face against any new expansion. Let us reconcile ourselves to the present reduction in values where not unnaturally low, and with moderate importation and universal economy strengthen our financial position. All this seems to be in the power of the Secretary. Is it not worth the effort? With a firm hand at the helm we may pass the dangerous breakers and reach the safe and open sea. Is not this our true policy?

KNICKERBOCKER.

NEW-YORK, *September* 30, 1873.

Letter No. III.

OUR PRESENT NEED.

No one, however interested in stock values, or in industrial or mercantile enterprises, will deny that the present need of the country at large is the movement of the crops from the interior to the sea-board, and their prompt shipment to the ready market which awaits them on the other side of the Atlantic. Though all crops will somewhat suffer from delay, we refer for the moment only to those to which delay may not only be injurious but ruinous. The cotton crop may wait its time, although it may be more profitable to the country that it should go rapidly forward. To it the question of early or late movement is after all only one of comparative profit. The grain and produce crops are not in the same situation. To these, every day's delay is fraught with incalculable danger. The present stoppage occurs at the very critical moment. Cotton may leave the Southern ports or our own at any period; there is no danger of ice-bound fleets upon the Atlantic, but the time for the inland transport of our Western product to the sea-board markets is necessarily limited. In these latitudes there is only one period for such transport, and that a short one, between the harvesting of the crops and the general closing of the canals.

Were we to-day, at the beginning of September, instead of the first days of October, we might wait in patience for a general return of confidence and the gradual release of currency to play its usual part in this most important portion of our foreign trade. There is an axiom current still among our older and conservative merchants, "that the true time to sell is when there is a wish to buy." And it is true of nations as of individuals. We have a great grain crop. The European nations allow that they are sadly in want of a large part of what we have to sell. How shall we give them that which they are so ready to take!

The recent stringency in *money*—we use the word deliberately, because currency is now our only money—since by our necessities, springing from the abnormal state of affairs into which war led us, gold is only as yet a standard of value—the recent stringency in money has already arrested the ordinary exchanges of produce for currency, which always take place at this season. To-day foreign exchange is quoted as "higher;" this means, that the produce already forwarded and ready for shipment has found shipment, and that the bills of exchange drawn against it have found buyers—but to how limited an extent! The extent is easily measured. The foreign bankers, relieved from the immediate pressure by just so much as their discounts of paper for their own or foreign account have been taken by the banks or note brokers—acting for their own or friends' account—have been able to use such relief in fresh purchases. The purchase of bankers' exchange by importers is not worth the naming. The importers, resting on their banks for their discounts, have surely not been permitted to use such discounts for much, if any thing, more than the payment of their obligations to such banks or the withdrawal of the engagements of their creditors endorsed by them.

Beyond this point there has been and there is no present relief to the dead-lock in exchange. Precisely as gold is held above its value, because there is no cash gold in the market, and no buyers at its present unreasonable price, so produce bills have advanced, because those on the market have been already absorbed by the funds which the foreign bankers, no longer timid as to the immediate future, have been willing to unlock from their strong boxes. But it may be safely said, that all the foreign bankers combined have not to-day the power to move one fortnight's, if even one week's, receipts of our crops. The business of a foreign exchange banker is not to use his own funds in the purchase of bills for remittance abroad and return in gold, but for the purchase of just so many bills as he may find sale for. He is the agent in the transaction, not the principal. He can only be the principal to the extent of his own available funds. Beyond this he may look for receipts of coin sent from abroad for investment here in bills at a low price against bills of lading. But this demands time. Have we the time to spare? Can the country safely wait for this "barter trade?" Will any ordinary release of currency provide the relief necessary in time, or before the closing of the canals? It is not necessary to touch upon the power of the rail-roads; we need *every* avenue for a cheap movement. The present stringency will make it costly enough in any event.

The Produce Exchange saw the difficulty early and appealed to the Secretary of the Treasury. In 1857 they appealed to the banks of New-York, who were then the masters of the currency under the State laws. The banks associated themselves and appointed an Exchange Committee, which went into the open market and bought the low bills, to a small extent, it is true, because our importers were largely debtors abroad, and the instant the foreign bankers saw that the banks were ready to purchase, they entered the market themselves. This, it is to be remembered, was after the banks suspended, when the whole community sanctioned that suspension, and when gold was at a slight premium.

To-day the banks are not in a similar situation. They are under positive engagements as national banks to the Government, and gold is far above par, nominally at least. The banks must put their own houses in order. Therefore, to the Secretary of the Treasury the Produce Exchange of New-York applies for aid, and the interior Produce Exchanges suspend all transactions until they receive that currency, to obtain which they are straining every nerve and drawing out every Eastern balance.

The Secretary replies that he would not if he could enter into any rivalry with the foreign bankers. Why need he enter into any rivalry ? Let him make an arrangement by Syndicate, if desirable, with BROWN BROTHERS & Co., DUNCAN, SHERMAN & Co., JOHN MUNROE & Co., DREXEL, MORGAN & Co., the WARDS, who are still the time-honored agents of the BARINGS, for the import of $20,000,000 to $25,000,000 of coin, and provide such currency as they may need here for immediate use in purchase of produce bills, or by other modes as they may elect to bring on the Western produce. The $44,000,000 reserve, which the President seems willing to use in imperative need, could not be better applied for the general interest. If the Secretary have not the authority, let him summon the Finance Committees of the Senate and House to endorse his request to the Executive to order such action, under their engagement to bring in a bill of indemnity at the next session of Congress. Such practice is usual in governments in times of national disaster. We will not refer here to the effect such action as this would have upon the restoration of specie payment. The Secretary need not hug his gold-bags and hesitate as to what premium his reserves of coin may be worth. The country will forgive him all the difference his hoard is worth above currency if by his action gold reaches par, and the American Eagle once more have its place not only in the American heart, but the American pocket.

KNICKERBOCKER.

NEW-YORK, *October* 2, 1873.

Letter No. IV.

SUBSTITUTION NOT CONTRACTION.

It is clear that, for the present at least, there is no excess of circulating medium—we may as well say of *currency*, because the circulating medium is now composed wholly of currency, in nearly equal proportions of greenbacks and national bank notes—the circulating medium, the measure by which all values are graded, consisting at the moment of seven hundred millions of notes. That there is a scarcity of currency to carry on the transactions of the country at this day, leads to the natural and not unfair inference, that the business of the country has "*grown up*" to the present amount of circulating medium.

As we have before stated, the business of the country was carried on in 1860 by a circulating medium of four hundred and fifty millions of dollars, of which two hundred millions, by official statement, were in State bank notes, and two hundred and fifty millions, by the estimate of those best fitted to judge, in coin. With this amount of circulating medium prices were at gold values and gold itself at par. When there is no demand for gold, except as a commodity—that is, when there is no demand for it as money to pay the indebtedness of this country to foreign countries—it must take the fate of all other commodities, and rise or fall as the circulating medium of the country is extended or diminished.

The experience of all nations has shown that just so far as the circulating medium is expanded prices rise, and so far as it is contracted prices fall. There can be no better illustration than that of the thermometer. The degrees are measured from freezing point to that where water boils, according to the length of the instrument. So with the circulating medium; double its extent and the prices measured by it double. Reduce it one-half and the prices measured by it fall one-half.

That we have not too large a circulating medium is clearly shown by the fact that there is now a scarcity of it. General prices are now reduced to gold prices, and, as this stringency becomes felt in every branch of trade, retail as well as wholesale, prices will not range above those that would range were we at specie payments.

The only value about which we are ignorant to-day is the value

of gold. Had the Secretary of the Treasury continued his sales instead of arresting them, we should have been in no uncertainty on
this subject to-day. Under the idea that this officer had become
alarmed about the strength of the Treasury—an odd idea enough
when the cable announced large shipments of coin to this side from
Europe—the gold brokers, whose business would be utterly de-
stroyed were gold to-day at par, made desperate efforts to raise the
price of gold. This spasmodic effort soon ran out its strength, and
gold, which advanced from 112 to 115⅜, has again fallen to 110.
We again repeat that we do not believe that five millions of gold
could to-day be put upon the market without its price falling to
par. With foreign exchanges in our favor, a great crop going forward, and large amounts of coin already on the way to this
country, there is little temptation to the speculator to risk his
money in the purchase of gold at any point above par.

We assert that gold is not worth more than par—a statement the
truth of which can only be established by the renewal of sales by
the Secretary, the only holder of gold to whom a fall is not an in-
jury. The great public advantage which will accrue from the decline of gold to par is so infinitely greater than the loss which may
accrue to the Treasury from the loss of the premium upon the stock
now held by it, that it seems almost an offence to the good sense of
the Secretary to suppose such a consideration to exist in his mind.

If gold be not worth more than par, then resumption may be made
without contraction; that is, without a contraction of the circulating
medium. Practical resumption means *substitution*, not contraction
—the substitution of coin for paper in our circulating medium. How
is this to be effected? In the first place evidently only by the
withdrawal of currency and the creation of a vacuum in the circulating medium, now wholly currency, into which gold, floating at
par, will flow and be absorbed. By just so much as currency is
diminished and gold fills its place will the circulating medium be
strengthened. So long as gold remains at par this process may continue. The Secretary can retire his greenbacks and gold will take
their place. This is the immediate need, and our present object is
to show that it can be reached without contraction. The experiment
is worth making. Let the Secretary put out his gold and ascertain
its value. That value will show the measure of our inflation, if such
there be. If it be not above par, as seems probable, it will be evi-
dent to the merest tyro in finance that the country has grown up to
its present circulating medium, and that the substitution of coin for
currency is now possible. When sufficient currency has been taken

out of and an equal amount of gold has entered into the circulating medium, *legal resumption* will follow as a matter of course, and all this without any disturbance of values or further shrinkage. So long as money is at seven per cent. in the financial centres, the Secretary can continue this process. With an easy money market nothing is more easy than such substitution of gold for greenbacks. So long as the exchanges remain favorable it can be rapidly effected. When money becomes dearer the process must be arrested. He must avoid the dangerous rock on which Mr. Secretary McCulloch wrecked his stiff bark. No business community will endure contraction when money is dear. But we hold that now contraction is not necessary. Substitution is not contraction. The measure of value is neither lengthened nor shortened. It is only strengthened.

Why should such an opportunity be neglected? Is not the experiment worth making when the possible advantages are considered? The renewal of the sales of gold by the Secretary is the first imperative step. By continuing the hoard of his Customs receipts he stands in the way of resumption. He is to-day the only block in the road to specie resumption. By his negative action in his arrest of sales of the surplus coin of the Treasury he is assuming a grave responsibility. Does he not see that his inaction gives time and occasion for a renewal of that speculative power which has already brought us into such serious difficulty. Let him so act that the coin now on its way from Europe will find its place in the vaults of our savings banks and the pockets of the people. Let us once more become familiar with the time-honored emblem of our national power. He may be sure that the American people will pardon him many shortcomings if he restore the national coin to general use. Until Congress meet, the Secretary holds this great power—the sustaining of the present unnatural value of gold or its restoration to the currency. *Can he hesitate?*

KNICKERBOCKER.

NEW-YORK, *October* 4, 1873.

Letter No. V.

NO FURTHER INFLATION.

THE crisis is passed—the panic has run its course; confidence is returning. There will be, doubtless, a great deal of individual suffering, a long train of minor disasters. It is impossible that it should be otherwise. Such is the unavoidable result of financial spasms. There will still be large and long-continued liquidations. Many needed and worthy enterprises must be for a period suspended, and new projects must be adjourned for a more favorable season. But the great and necessary business of the country is gradually renewing its former current. The prudent still husband their resources, and move with caution. Others, more venturesome, only wait the returning breeze to spread full sail once more.

Severe as the lesson has been to all—sudden as the awakening from a blind trust in the perpetual postponement of the day of settlement under the much-vaunted merits of paper-money—it is a question whether even yet that warning has aroused the public mind to a true sense of the danger, or brought fairly home to the national conscience the changeless, incontrovertible truth, that so long as we make one of the family of commercial nations, we must use that money which is the common money of the world, or find no relief from the common fund of that money in the time of need.

Had our circulating medium been of this character, or approached to this standard—that is to say, did it now consist of equal parts of coin and paper—the contraction caused by the recent sudden lapse of confidence, the withdrawal of currency and impaired power to perform its usual functions of that which remained, would have inevitably and immediately attracted an addition to its store of coin from foreign nations. This not being possible, the business of the country was compelled to contract itself to the amount of currency still left free. There was no hope of aid from foreign sources. The only money with which foreign nations could have aided us in our need, gold and silver, are no longer money with us—they would only have served as an additional sum of commodities to be dealt in, bought and sold with the very currency which proved insufficient for already existing transactions, or rather such part of it as a timorous public still left free for such purposes.

In a similar situation of affairs in England or France, such stringencies are treated in a simple way. The price of money is raised. The raising of the bank rate of discount is equivalent to a rise in such price. Gold and silver, like all other commodities, seek the market where they are most wanted and find most profitable employment. From every quarter the current of money sets in to the point where it may be used to best advantage, and business transactions contracting, the equilibrium is soon restored. The true amount of circulating medium as a measure of transactions is again reached, and trade resumes its movement under correct and normal conditions. Confidence cheapens money, and the floating capital which has corrected the false relations of values awaits another favorable investment. This natural movement can only take place in countries where the circulating medium is strong, because largely consisting of gold and silver, and where transactions in money are left free and unfettered by restrictive laws, like those of Usury, which, to our cost, still retain their place on our statute-book. The Bank of England makes money dear by raising its rate of discount, or rather raises its rate of discount as money becomes or threatens to become scarce. Our unfortunate banks can only make money dear by denying it; while, on the other hand, so soon as they take this course, their customers withhold from them their usual deposits, because they can use their money more profitably in the open market, the Usury laws as between man and man being little more than a dead letter.

The entire inadequateness of a circulating medium consisting *solely of paper*, has been absolutely demonstrated in the recent crisis. To what extent prices would have fallen, and what further terrible calamity would have been endured, but for the happy chance that there was a moderate sum of currency at the disposal of the Treasury at the critical moment, need not now be inquired. He who has fallen half way down a precipice takes more thought as to how he may again reach the surface than of the extent of the deeper depth below.

Yet, strange as it may seem, there is at this very moment a plot forming to press upon Congress at its next session the issue of *one hundred millions more of greenbacks*, under the plea that we cannot carry on the business of the country with the present sum of seven hundred millions. There is no secrecy about this scheme; it is talked of in more than one influential quarter. What is equally serious—the press, which of late has been almost unanimous in its urgent demand for measures toward resumption, has fallen under the spell, and no more is heard about specie resumption.

Are men crazy that they propose such schemes? More inflation! Another hundred millions of irredeemable money! Where is this to end? When this hundred millions is fairly afloat, what then? Why then another and another, until our worthless currency will have about as much purchasing power as the old French assignat, or the promises of the darkest hour of our revolutionary struggle. For several years, indeed ever since the power of contraction was taken away from the Secretary, the country has been lured on by the delusive promise that when we had "grown up" to the present circulating medium, specie payment would be resumed; and now that the country *has* grown up to the present circulating medium, it is to be deprived of the reward of its patient sacrifice, and is told by these patent currency doctors that it must "grow up" to a medium one hundred millions greater than that now existing. When are we to stop "growing up?"

I greatly mistake the temper of our people if they will for a moment sanction such a breach of faith as this. There are signs on every side that they are awakening to a thorough understanding of this question. They begin to see that national expansion brings in its train individual expansion; that a diluted currency brings watered stocks. Already, in this State, one of the great political parties has put forward, as the very corner-stone of its platform, the imperative need of a return to specie payment.

If it be true that the business of the country has grown up to the present circulating medium, it is now the time to strengthen that circulating medium by a large introduction of coin. As we have already shown, *no contraction is necessary*, only a gradual withdrawal by the Secretary of the greenback currency; when gold is at par it will flow into the vacuum thus created. In other words, a substitution of coin for greenbacks. When the greenbacks have been withdrawn, and gold has taken their place, legal resumption may take place. If, then, the country prefer to replace the national bank currency by greenbacks, made convertible into coin at the Sub-Treasuries, the exchange may be made by a simple process. The Secretary could redeem, with this convertible currency, the bonds now lodged with the Treasury by the national banks, and call in and cancel the bank notes. The United States would then possess the best circulating medium in the world, half in Government notes, equivalent to and convertible into coin, and the other half in gold and silver; while banks would be left to their legitimate business of discount and deposit unrestricted by law. But the discussion of this question is premature. The feasibility of such an exchange is only mentioned, because a large part of our population look with aversion upon any withdrawal of greenbacks if it is to be final—who prefer the Government to the bank issue, and object to any plan of finance which enables one class of individuals to profit by the currency which the whole people make use of. Such profits, they assert, belong to the whole people. Nowhere is class legislation so dreaded and detested as here.

The immediate question is, have we "grown up" to the present circulating medium? If we have not, we surely want *no more inflation* until we do grow up to it. If we have, we want the first step to the introduction of gold into that medium. I hold that we are ready for such a step now. If there is no excess of currency and no foreign demand for coin, gold should be at par, and other values at gold values. If the Secretary will resume his sales of gold, this point will be soon established.

No withdrawal of currency should take place until gold be at par. The country is not in a situation or humor to endure any more of the "heroic treatment" of Mr. Secretary McCulloch. It is now universally accepted that the growing-up process is to be the only treatment. In pursuing his present policy, the Secretary, instead of aiding in the establishment of the true value of gold, stands absolutely in its way. The Canadian bankers, who are understood to be the holders of the greater part of the cash gold in the market, must laugh in their sleeves while the duty-paying importer gradually relieves them of their stock at the rate of two or three millions each week, and the Secretary absorbs their sales in his Customs receipts, and sustains the market for our provincial friends. Is this Fabian policy of the Secretary's own conception? Whoever may be its prompters, the foreign bankers and gold speculators are the only persons who find their account in the fictitious value of gold. Finance is not an exact science, and no one knows precisely how much cash gold there is on the market, or what price a round sum, say of five millions, would command. The Secretary holds the solution of this problem in his own hand. His silence can only be explained on the theory of the Eastern proverb, that "silence is golden."

Everything favors resumption now. Our imports from the 1st of January to 1st of October, 1873, show a falling off of $27,000,000 from those of the same period last year; our exports an excess during the same period of over $48,000,000, an improvement in our favor, in exact figures, of $75,871,472 for the first three-quarters of the year 1873. Of specie, the exports have been $41,523,011, in 1873, against $59,075,264 in 1872, and $69,702,111 in 1871. This ratio of improvement will be daily increasing for the remaining quarter. The recent crisis has arrested imports, except of coin, to a very great extent, while every day's news from Great Britain and the Continent points to even larger takings of our breadstuffs than had been supposed. The shortness of the wheat crop seems to be not only local but continental. A carefully considered article in the London *Saturday Review* on the "Wheat Crop," estimates "that England's deficit is probably 12,000,000, and that of France 6,000,000, or together

18,000,000 quarters. England, the only buyer in the past year, has imported from all other countries, France included, nearly 13,000,000 quarters of wheat. The two countries now require that quantity, and fully 5,000,000 more, between them. The question is, can this quantity be obtained ? * * It is too much, however, to expect America to more than double her exportation of last year. It is improbable, if not impossible, that she can so do. Either France or England must then go short. There will be active competition between the merchants of the two nations wherever wheat is to be had, and the result of the competition will be, to raise prices. Bread must be dear. Whoever goes short, this country (England) will not starve; but we shall have to pay a high price for our loaf."

In the compensation of nature, their suffering is our prosperity. The day is not distant since Great Britain profited by our calamity. For a great part of their wants, England and France must pay us specie. We will therefore not only retain our own large production, but receive a considerable additional supply. Now is our chance. If we neglect this opportunity to restore our national finances to a sound specie basis, we shall incur, and as surely receive, the contempt of mankind. We may as well return to the aboriginal currency at once, and establish a *wampum* factory at the capital. Better this than continue the farce of exchanging paper promises, which we have no intention of performing, now or hereafter, and solemnly calling them dollars.

Let us have no more inflation.

KNICKERBOCKER.

NEW-YORK, *October* 6, 1873.

Letter No. VI.

GRADUAL RESUMPTION.

THE discussion of the question of a return to specie payment has now passed from the narrow field of bank parlors and merchants' counting-rooms to the broad forum of public opinion. It is no longer possible to put off or stifle this discussion. It will not " down " at any man's bidding. It is to the press of the country that the people look for light and counsel. This is the time to settle some of the main points in the argument. When the premises of any proposition are clearly proven, and taken as proven, the conclusions which derive from such premises are sure to lodge themselves in the public mind. Public action soon results, for though those charged with our Government may fail sometimes to lead public opinion, they rarely hesitate to follow it when clearly expressed.

The questions now before the public are these: Are specie payments desirable? Are specie payments now practicable? How shall the experiment be made?

That there is an earnest desire for a return to the use of coin in our currency cannot be now denied. In every quarter this feeling is shown. The country has heard in the last few days the opinions of the two Senators from Ohio, one on the Democratic, the other on the Republican side. The argument is made to the people of Ohio and the Western States. The final settlement of the question rests in Western hands. They hold to-day, and will hold for a long period, the balance of power on this continent. Every argument addressed to them from authoritative sources must be fairly listened to, fairly weighed, and fairly answered. The question must not be permitted to pass wholly into the domain of political inquiry. It must not be confined within party limits. Buyers and sellers trade with each other without thought as to each other's political views. The coin which should be the standard of value in their dealings has no party color.

Mr. Senator SHERMAN, in his recent speech, made this important admission: "There are some defects in our banking system. The first is that a greenback, although mighty good, is not quite so good as gold." And again: "We can go back to specie payments—we can go back until our money is equivalent to gold and silver coin, and then we have the best currency in the world." While the Senator proposes no plan to make the currency as "good as gold," he affirms in the plainest way that "in all ages and in all countries it has got to be an axiom in financial matters, that gold alone is the standard of value, and the planetary laws which govern the universe are not more fixed and absolute in their sway than that law which demands that every thing must be measured by the gold standard." Such are the weighty, positive declarations of one of the Republican leaders. On the other hand, his colleague and political antagonist, the Democratic Senator from the same State, Mr. THURMAN, while declaring "that he is in favor of a specie currency, or a currency convertible into specie," and expressing the "belief that the business of the country can never be carried on with an irredeemable paper currency," is as silent as Mr. SHERMAN as to the means by which this convertibility or equalization of values of coin and paper may be established.

But here the resemblance between the views of these distinguished gentlemen ceases. Mr. THURMAN goes on in the strongest terms to deprecate the "immediate resumption" of specie payments as dangerous in the extreme, and calculated "to have a most crushing effect upon the people of the debtor States." Both of these gentlemen fairly and squarely declare their belief that specie payments are desirable and needful. There is nothing to controvert in the argument of either. In answer to that of Mr. SHERMAN, it need only be stated that no resumption can take place until the circulating medium, now wholly paper, has been very greatly strengthened in some manner. He would doubtless say by putting coin along side of it, while the sounder view seems to be that the true manner is by partial withdrawal of currency and substitution of coin in its place. To that of Mr. THURMAN, it is only necessary to reply that there is no such thing possible as the "immediate resumption of specie payments." He must be mad indeed who can for a moment imagine that the Government or the people can solemnly legislate or declare that they will hereafter pay specie to all who demand it, when the proportion of specie in their control to the extent of the currency promises afloat is in the present ratio. It is not worth while here to reply to the bold theory once put out, that all that was necessary for resumption was "to resume." The difficulty is to *stay resumed*. The financial history of nations shows no record of any people that have been able to float any considerable amount of currency with even an equal amount of coin to the circulating medium. There can be no other than gradual resumption by the substitution of coin for a part of the currency. As this substitution will in no manner change the amount of circulating medium, there will be no contraction, and Mr. THURMAN's fears as to the change of relation between debtor and creditor may be dismissed as idle and groundless.

The measure of values is the circulating medium of a country—the values so measured rise or fall, as the measure itself is enlarged or lessened. Gold is only a standard as it is used as a standard. Were it not for our intercourse with foreign nations we should have no use for it except in the arts, and Gold Boards and Sub-Treasuries would be needless. But as yet, the European and Asiatic nations have not adopted the last American conception, that gold is a "relic of barbarism," to be tabooed by all civilized nations, and they still insist on payment in gold for the balance of account between their sales to us and our purchases from them. Now, so long as we content ourselves to receive at home among ourselves a paper currency in place of coin, and to pay our foreign creditors in gold and silver, we may do so ; only as their money is not our money, we need not expect that aid which they mutually extend to each other in times of distress. We have placed ourselves out of the pale of their finance.

The prices of the articles we exchange among ourselves, giving and taking this paper money as the medium of transactions, will rise and fall as we increase or diminish the amount of such paper money ; or if we do neither, but hold the amount at a fixed limit, prices will fall, as the increasing business of the country consequent on its rapid development and prosperity causes an increased demand for the currency itself. That is what is called the "growing up" process. When the currency is not in excess, prices should not rule above those which prevail when gold is at par. And here it must not be lost sight of, that present gold prices are not those which ruled before the war, either here or in any part of the world. Prices have risen every where ; in Europe and Asia as well as in America. The enormous increase in the world's store of gold since 1848 has changed the financial face of the world, and caused a general advance in values to keep pace with the increase in the measure of values. This advance has been still further stimulated by the rapidity of modern communication, which has greatly reduced the necessity of any considerable movement of coin itself, and left nearly the entire sum existing at the free service of commercial exchanges. No such fall in prices here as many have feared need be looked for. The fact of a general rise abroad will be readily acknowledged by all those who have recently visited the Continent. Our fall need only meet that rise.

For many years the amount of our circulating medium has been in excess of the reasonable needs of the country. It is now claimed, and it seems justly, that the business of the country fully demands its present medium of seven hundred millions. There must, therefore, be no contraction of this medium. There must only be a substitution of gold for a part of that medium. This is *gradual resumption*. This is the only time since the close of the war when the condition of our foreign exchanges has permitted a serious thought of the possibility of such a substitution. Nothing but the great improvement in our situation toward foreign countries, and the certainty that for a considerable period this improvement must continue in a largely-increasing ratio, renders such a plan practicable to-day.

After long suspension, in which values, no longer measured by a gold standard, become irregular and unsettled, an immediate restoration of their true relations is difficult and unequal. It was a saying of that wisest and most sagacious of American statesmen, ALBERT GALLATIN, the financial Nestor by whose counsels the country was led through the revulsion of 1837 up to specie payment, " that the agony of resumption is far more terrible than the agony of suspension;" that it is harder to submit to a loss which may be avoided, or postponed, or perhaps shifted to another's shoulders, to aid resumption, than to far greater losses to avoid suspension. The moral tone, once impaired, is with difficulty restored, either in individuals or communities.

Fortunately, there is no need of such suffering now. The worst has been rapidly passed. The contraction of values has been sharp and sudden, but thorough. The deposite line of the New-York banks alone has fallen off $51,000,000 since the 13th September, a contraction of twenty-five per cent. There can be no further contraction. There will be no further general decline in values. There will be surely an equalization between those which have fallen too low and those which have not yet felt their share of the depression. It may safely be said that no values have wholly escaped. What are we to reap from this sudden restoration of true values ? Shall we hold steady where we are, and gradually recover our old financial standing by gradual resumption, or shall we drift along through another expansion and another inflation, to another panic ? Can there be any hesitation ? Surely, we will choose the better path—that which leads to national honor and sure prosperity. The long-promised day has at last dawned—the day when, by ten years of unexampled prosperity, the business of the country has grown up to the full measure of the circulating medium. Shall we not now endeavor to harmonize our system with the systems of all other civilized nations—to return to gold as a standard of values ?

It has been in the power of the Secretary of the Treasury at any time since the beginning of the panic, since the 17th September, to ascertain the value of gold—to enable the country to see and to know just how much difference really exists between the value of our currency and of coin—to fix precisely the excess of our circulating medium. What relief it would have afforded to the country to know that it was on the verge of specie payment—that at last there was to be a certain and definite element in our finances—what a consolation for it in its hours of suffering! It has not suited the Secretary to adopt this course.

It has been also in the power of the Secretary to uphold the price of gold, and sustain the hands of those whose business is a speculation in its changing values. No positive interference was necessary —the country would not have brooked such interference. He had only to withdraw the sales of gold he had advertised; to listen in silence, without demur, to the rumors of the dangers and embarrassments of the Treasury, by which the speculators bolstered their speculations upon nominal transactions; and finally, as confidence was renewed, and importers commenced to withdraw their merchandise, to absorb and hold his customs receipts, and thus help to maintain the artificial price. This has been the course of the Secretary.

The country cares little now for what he does. The matter has passed beyond his control. He had the power to lead the movement, to direct it in the proper path. The gold now on its way here is pouring daily into the mint for coinage. Had the Secretary shown any courage, the greater part of the ten millions which it is announced must pass through new coinage, would go directly into the hands of the people. All the gold on the way to this country must find a market here. Who can hold it? The foreign bankers have not the power if they have the inclination. The acceptances of the best of them, even ninety-day bills, cannot find takers at one and a quarter per cent. per month—sixteen per cent. per annum. Their credit is undoubted, but their available means are already exhausted in the purchase of produce bills. Their credit will not move the produce now on the market. They must wait before they can renew their purchases, until they find a demand for their bills which, as yet, comes slowly from importers, or receive coin from abroad.

It is greatly to be regretted that some means were not devised by the Secretary to import gold through a syndicate of bankers, and to place an immediate and large sum—twenty to twenty-five millions of currency—in their hands for use in the purchase of produce bills. The relief to the West would have been instant, and the general effect salutary. We could then have marketed a great part of the crops before frost, or at least brought it to tidewater. Already there are signs of an early Winter. Snow fell in Pennsylvania yesterday.

The coin must come, and gold will fall to par in spite of the Secretary. His brief authority will be powerless to sustain the price against arrivals for a market, and none will feel tempted to buy gold against such importations as are now promised. The Secretary has been measured in the balance and found wanting. Never in the history of our country has so great an occasion been so hopelessly neglected. Whatever other fame the Secretary may achieve, that of a finance minister has passed from him forever. When gold falls to par, and there is no longer profit or hope of profit in holding it, it will pass from hand to hand as of old. *But this is not resumption,* nor yet a single step toward it. It can only be held in the currency by the provision of a place for its use. This can only come from legislation. The appeal will be taken from the Secretary to Congress. When this important session is opened, there will be found two distinct propositions awaiting its approval, and the country marshaled behind the one or the other in columns in which political opinions will have no place. From the one will rise the cry for more inflation, more greenbacks; from the other a stern demand for a gradual approach to coin. There need be no doubt of the people's position. Every man who lives by his daily labor—the bone and sinew of the country, the American artisan, the Irish laborer, the German agriculturist—has an immediate daily interest in a return of specie payment; only let it be made clear to them that there is to be *immediate resumption,* no contraction and suffering, but only a gradual and careful substitution of coin for paper, continued when gold is at par and money is plenty, arrested when either gold advances or money becomes dear, and there can be no division of opinion.

It is now of the greatest importance to fully put before the people the entire feasibility of this plan of *gradual resumption,* and to destroy the popular impression that gold prices mean ruin. It is a sad thing, indeed, that the very word " specie-payment " has been so used before the people that it has become as much a terror as the red flag to France—a terrible banner to be waved before the eyes of the people on every occasion when the interests of a class are to be protected or sustained at the expense of the whole.

If the inflationists are allowed to have their way they will so corrupt the public conscience that the day may not be distant when resumptionists will fare as badly as abolitionists, in a time not yet beyond our memory; and one who expresses a doubt about the miraculous virtues of paper money be chased about the streets as those other sufferers, who dared to doubt the divine origin of the institution of human slavery. *Dii avertite omen !*

KNICKERBOCKER.

NEW-YORK, *October* 8, 1873.

/

Letter No. VII.

THE APPROACH TO SPECIE PAYMENT.

From the close of its war it has been the policy of the Government, under the Republican administration, to restore specie payment to the country.

Now that this policy is on the verge of success, it is not unprofitable to look over the extent of the ground already traveled, and to note with what steady and firm courage it has been pursued, so the country may better measure the distance yet to be gone over, and nerve itself for the last and crowning effort.

Mr. Secretary McCulloch, in his able and lucid report of 1867, states the public debt of the United States to have reached its highest point on the 31st August, 1865, when it stood at $2,757,689,571 43. The October statement of Mr. Secretary Richardson states the total indebtedness, on the 31st September, 1873, as at $2,138,793,898 17. In both statements the cash in the Treasury is deducted. A total reduction in eight years of $618,895,673 26. The history of the finances of the world shows no record of any such remarkable feat as this. Alone it stands, and will stand to the honor of the able men who have conducted the national finances, and an imperishable proof of the boundless resources of the country itself and the inflexible courage of our people.

It is upon these resources and this courage that the hope of a finish of the labor in an early return to specie payment is now founded.

A short analysis will show of what the debt consisted at the time of its greatest extent, and to what it is now reduced.

On the 31st of August, 1865, there were of

Funded and matured debt,.	$1,111,071,211 89
Seven-thirty notes,.........	830,000,000 00
Temporary loans, certificates of indebtedness, &c.,............	443,220,103 16
United States greenbacks and fractional currency,............	459,505,311 51
	$2,843,796,626 56
Less cash in Treasury, minus unpaid requisitions,............	86,107,055 13
Total debt United States,.....................	$2,757,689,571 43

On the 31st September, 1873, there were of

Funded debt, interest in coin,..........................	$1,723,567,500 00
Funded debt, in lawful money,.........................	14,000,000 00
Matured debt,..	15,756,130 26
Certificates of indebtedness,.............................	678,000 00
Certificates of deposits,..................................	11,250,000 00
Greenbacks and fractional currency,......................	402,309,134 03
Unpaid interest,...	32,083,523 46
	$2,199,644,287 75
Less cash in Treasury,...................................	60,850,389 58
Total debt United States,.........................	$2,138,793,898 17

The first measure of Mr. Secretary McCulloch, on taking charge of the Department, was to get rid of the floating debt, which, in its various forms, clogged the wheels of the Treasury, by paying off what was possible and funding the balance. His next, to fund the general debt as far as practicable. For this great measure of converting the $800,000,000 of seven-thirty obligations into gold bonds he has been as widely blamed on the one hand as he has been praised on the other. "But for this step," a recent critic has remarked of him, " he might have been called a great finance minister." But this very measure is the great measure of his career. By it he brought American credit up to its present high standard in the money markets of the world. Seeing from the first that sooner or later the finances of the United States must be put upon the same level as those of other nations, and aware of the difficulties in the way of a return to specie payment, he resolved to place the bonds of the Government *at once* upon that basis. No greater proof of the wisdom of his policy need be asked, than the favored and firm hold that these obligations now have among foreign nations—a hold they could not have maintained on a currency basis. Satisfied as the European holder might be as to the ultimate value of his investment, he looked naturally to a specific coin interest. This the conversion from the currency obligation to a gold bond provided.

The next step of the Secretary was a resolute effort to contract the currency, and bring it back as far as possible to its normal state; in other words, to reduce the circulating medium to the sum absolutely necessary for the transaction of the business of the country.

By reference to the report of August 31, 1865, it will be found that the circulating medium then consisted of

United States notes, greenbacks and fractional currency,....... $459,505,311 51
National Bank notes and State Bank issues, as by Comptroller's
report, October 1, 1865,.................................. 250,189,478 00

Total,... $709,694,789 51

To this amount must be added the sum of five per cent. legal
tender notes, and of certificates of indebtedness, &c., shown as above
to amount to $443,220,103 16, in all a sum of $1,152,914,892 67.
This, then, was the circulating medium of the country at the time
of its greatest expansion; by it all prices were measured.

After the taking in of the various kinds of certificates, all which
served the purpose of currency in one form or another, Mr. McCulloch begun to take in the greenbacks themselves, and continued
until in December, 1867, Congress formally stopped any further contraction. From the 1st of August to the 15th November, 1867, the
time of his greatest contraction of greenbacks, the complaints of the
Western country were unceasing against the policy of the Secretary, and, indeed, if there be a fault to be found with his direction
of the finances, it is in that he clung so inflexibly to a fixed and
unyielding policy. He insisted upon contraction without regard to
the demands of the trade of the country or the position of the money
market. From his experience future Secretaries may take note, that
while no complaints are likely to arise against contraction when
money is cheap, no country which, by the representative system,
holds the power in its own hands, and can confine the action of its
finance ministers within the limits of its will, is likely to consent to
a contraction of its currency when money is dear.

The Treasury statement of July, 1868, shows to what extent the
circulating medium had been then contracted. It then consisted of—

United States notes, greenbacks and fractional currency,....... $388,768,674 75
National bank notes outstanding 1st November, 1867,......... 299,103,996 00

Total,... $687,872,670 75

To which we add the sum of temporary loan certificates and other
notes serving the purposes of currency, amounting to $92,687,442 64,
and the sum of the circulating medium will be found to have then
reached $780,560,113 39, and shows a contraction by the Secretary
of $372,354,779 28 in its total amount. This was pointed out during
the debates of the Board of Trade Convention which met at Boston
in the spring of 1868. An article in the *Atlantic Monthly*, for May
of this year, renews the same argument.

This was the *first approach to specie payment.* The country at large had felt the pressure of the screw, but had not been able to discern precisely from what quarter the pinch came, the contraction being partly those outside forms of Treasury obligations, which, though not currency in the strict acceptation of the word, were still used as such in the larger transactions of trade and financial exchange. When, in a time of general pressure, the currency itself became the subject of the pruning knife, the country not only felt the knife, but saw how it was handled, and refused to submit longer to the " heroic treatment." Up to this period, July, 1868, it will be seen that the debt itself, that is, the funded debt, though materially re-arranged, had been slightly increased. In July, 1865, the sum of the indebtedness not used as currency was $1,931,071,211 89, of which $830,000,000 were 7-30 Treasury notes. In 1868, July, the same class of debt reached $2,154,864,847 28, of which $177,000,000 and some fractions of 7-30 Treasury notes, an increase of $200,000,000. During all this period the entire indebtedness of the Treasury had fallen from $2,757,689,571 43 to $2,636,320,964 67, a decrease of $121,368,606 76.

Checked in his efforts to approach further to specie payment by direct contraction, the country having distinctly shown its determination to " grow up " to the existing circulation without further change, Mr. McCulloch set himself to work to reduce the debt itself. The statement of July, 1869, made shortly after he left office, returned the amount as then outstanding at $2,489,002,480 58, a total reduction since the inauguration of his policy of $294,423,398 63. The country will some day recognise the full measure of the services that this brave Secretary rendered in the beginning of such a wise policy.

The administration of Gen. GRANT under Mr. BOUTWELL followed the policy of its predecessors, leaving the currency untouched and continuing the approach to specie payment by the collateral road of a reduction of Government indebtedness. On the 1st of July, 1873, there had been a still further reduction of indebtedness of $339,038,607.

Mr. Secretary RICHARDSON has continued faithfully and bravely in the same direction. His reduction since July alone reaches the sum of $11,169,975; the total reduction since 1865 reaching the sum of $618,895,673 26, and leaving the debt within the easily-managed figure of a little over two thousand millions. This has been the *second approach to specie payment.*

The country is now ready for the third great series of steps toward resumption. If we have now " grown up " to the sum of our circulating medium, now is the time to prepare to introduce some solid strength into that medium. When gold and currency float at par together and money is abundant, a gradual withdrawal of currency will not be felt since gold will fill its place. Values will remain unchanged and resumption will gradually become possible. When gold has fairly taken its place in sufficient amount to warrant the experiment, there may be legal resumption, and the people may then decide which of the two currencies they prefer—greenbacks or national bank notes. The exchange of greenbacks for the national bank currency will be easy. The Treasury will only have to redeem the bonds on which the bank issues are based, paying for them with a convertible greenback currency, which would thus become the only paper money in circulation, and by the same process extinguish $350,000,000 of the United States debt—a desirable financial operation in itself.

Are we ready for this last step—the *third approach to specie payment?* It seems that we are not far from it. Our exports are enormous; our imports are light, and promise to be small for some time. The credit of importers will not allow of other result—they perforce must contract their business. Gold is falling, and would long ago have touched par, or a point near it, but for the mistaken policy of the Secretary. The October statement shows that while his gold balance fell from $87,000,000, as it stood Sept. 1st, to $80,000,000, as on the 1st of October, the portion of the coin belonging to the Treasury increased from $42,000,000 to $46,000,000, and that while the coin certificates were called for to the extent of $10,000,000, the real gold strength of the Treasury increased $4,000,000—about the amount of his customs receipts.

Before the meeting of Congress gold will probably be floating at par. The Treasury can only absorb a moderate amount—the balance must take its chance of the market. It cannot escape us, unless we again inflate the currency. The Secretary may yet find no better use for his coin than to redeem the amount taken from the famous reserve. He cannot use it to a better purpose.

It will be for Congress to make such legislation as will then authorize the Secretary to withdraw his greenbacks so fast as coin is at hand to replace them,' and thus take the final step in the approach to specie payment.

There can be no doubt that the Republican Administration, which has so steadily held this object in view, will not now fail either in the wisdom or the courage to complete its work.

KNICKERBOCKER.

New-York, *October* 10, 1873.

Letter No. VIII.

THE TRUE PLAN FOR RESUMPTION.

The temper of the Press which, if not always ready to lead, is sure to follow the drift of public opinion, shows clearly that the question of specie payment has lodged itself in the mind of the people. There is a wide-spread belief in the present practicability of specie payment, and symptoms of an anxious longing for this most desirable result, accompanied, it is not to be denied, with many a sign of dread of the suffering it may entail. There is an instinctive fear that specie payment means decline in values, loss of property, falling perhaps where least looked for; with all this a growing determination to face the danger, to grapple with it, and overcome it.

Specie payment will be the one measure of the coming session. It is already announced that President Grant will make this subject a part of his Message to Congress, and recommend some practical measure for its consideration. The question is not, then, of the merits of specie payment, but of the plan by which it may be carried into effect.

Several plans of resumption have been brought forward.

The first plan, that to which all nations have hitherto had resort in similar stress, was that originally proposed by Mr. Secretary McCulloch in his report of 30th November, 1867. He stated that he would not fix the exact time of resumption, yet that under favorable circumstances " it should not be delayed beyond the 1st January, or, at the furthest, the 1st July, 1869." To this end as a chief measure he proposed to Congress " the funding or payment of the balance of interest-bearing notes and a *continued contraction of the paper currency.*" But while Congress listened with willing ear to his wise scheme of taking up the interest-bearing notes, they absolutely denied his urgent request to continue his contraction policy, and passed a law to suspend the further reduction of the currency. It was resolved upon to wait until the progress and prosperity of the country had expanded its business to the measure of its currency—until it had " grown up " to it.

It is worth while now only to mark at what stage of his contraction policy Mr. Secretary McCulloch thought that specie payment might be resumed, and thereby to estimate how much paper currency he judged could be safely floated. He had previously stated in his December report, 1865, that it would not be necessary to retire more than one, or at most two hundred millions of United States notes before the desired result would be obtained. The amount of paper circulation, he stated in the same report to be, on Oct. 31, 1865 :

United States notes and fractional currency,	$454,218,038 20
Notes of national banks,	185,000,000 00
State bank notes outstanding,	65,000,000 00
Total,	$704,218,038 20

In other words, Mr. McCulloch was then of opinion that the par of coin could be maintained with a paper circulation of $500,000,000. In November, 1867, when he expressed the opinion that resumption could take place at the furthest the 1st July, 1869, the currency stood, by his statement, at—

United States notes and fractional currency,	$387,871,477 39
National bank notes,	299,103,996 00
Total,	$686,975,473 39

But a condition of resumption in his policy was a still further contraction of the paper issues. He could scarcely expect Congress to permit him to contract faster than he had already contracted. The country was already wincing under the severity of the process. From the 30th November, 1867, to the 1st July, 1869, the date he fixed for possible resumption, a period of nineteen months, he could not have hoped to contract at a greater rate than four millions per month ; a full sum of seventy-six millions. The sum of paper money would then be that last stated, less seventy-six millions; in other words, say six hundred million dollars. It will be seen that the Secretary made an allowance for the growth of the country from 1865 to 1869, and its consequent need of an increased circulating medium, by the advance in the sum of paper currency which he estimated that the country could float at a par of coin by one hundred millions—that is, from five to six hundred millions.

If this view be correct, and a similar advance of 100 millions for the four years from 1869 to 1873, (his estimate was of an advance of 100 millions for the four years from 1865 to 1869,) be now allowed as not unreasonable, then we have the sum of 700 millions as the precise measure of the amount of paper currency which, in his view, can now be floated on a par with coin—at least, if present inferences may be drawn from his past opinions. The precise measure of our present currency may as well be stated:

United States greenbacks and fractional currency, Oct. 1, 1873,. $402,309,134 03
National bank notes, Feb. 28, 1873,...................... 336,292,459 00

Total,...................................... $738,601,593 03

From what may be gathered from the reports of Mr. McCulloch, his plan of a return to specie payment was contraction to a certain point, which has been stated, and then *resumption by the Treasury on the basis of a gold reserve in its vaults.* The national banks would have followed perforce, or, falling under the ban of the law, have been wound up and passed out of existence.

The plan of Mr. Greeley for immediate resumption was based on the same theory of Treasury resumption. In his financial address at Louisville, September 22, 1872, during the political canvass which preceded the last election, he said: "My opinion was, years ago, and I have seen no reason to change it, that when we had one hundred and twenty-five millions of money in the Treasury, mainly gold, and when we had a revenue exceeding the necessary outlays of the Treasury by more than one hundred millions per annum, we were then in a condition to resume specie payments; that if the Government had chosen to say 'we will resume, we will take our greenbacks and will receive them as gold,' there would have been no difficulty in making that resumption. Under that state of affairs I have seen the Bank of England resume." Mr. Greeley not only omitted to state that the Government had come into solemn engagement with every taker of its bonds to collect its customs in coin for the secure payment of their interest, and that a breach of faith, even in a partial abandonment of this pledge, would seriously injure the national credit, but he further forgot that when the Bank of England resumed, it was to make good in coin a currency of 21 million pounds sterling—100 millions of dollars—the amount of its paper currency, outstanding at the day of its greatest expansion, and not 400 millions, as our Treasury would have been forced to do, and this, too, in a country where gold is always abundant and which is in close proximity to the great gold money markets of the world—Paris, Amsterdam, Frankfort and Vienna —while, on the other hand, coin has for years been gradually driven out of the United States, and the viciousness of our system has placed us out of the reach of foreign aid and sympathy.

The third plan is that of Mr. Senator SHERMAN, who introduced into the Senate, on the 11th July, 1868, a bill for the funding of the national debt and for the conversion of the notes of the United States. This provided for conversion at the will of any holder of United States notes, (greenbacks,) to the amount of $1,000, or any multiple of $1,000, into bonds for an equal amount, and that any holder of the bonds might demand payment of the same by the Treasury, unless the amount of notes outstanding shall be equal to 400 millions —such process to cease after the resumption of specie payments by the United States. To this was added a section giving legality to contracts made specifically in coin. The advantages of this plan were more apparent' than real, and they grew smaller, as, by the gradual reduction of the funded debt, it passed into firmer and more secure holding. The holders of the debt during the recent crisis were not, to any great extent, willing to convert their bonds into currency when they had the opportunity, by the sale of bonds to the Secretary. The demand for such conversion came chiefly from the savings banks, who, having immediate engagements to fulfill, the possible extent of which they could not measure, made such conversion, but locked up the currency. It afforded little relief to the general community.

It must be also observed that the limit, 400 millions, set up as the barrier, which should not be passed, in such conversion of bonds into currency, is not far distant. Mr. SHERMAN will no doubt also now allow that the country has grown up to the amount of currency, 700 millions, which he considered to be thirty-five per cent. in excess of our needs in 1869. This ingenious plan of convertibility back and forth of bonds into currency and currency into bonds for the purpose of furnishing *flexibility* to the currency, is the corner-stone of the free-banking law project.

In January, 1869, Mr. SHERMAN put forward a further plan.

He then proposed, in addition to the legalization of gold contracts and the extension of this system to the national banks, a grant to the banks of the authority to issue gold notes equal to sixty-five per cent. of the value of United States bonds deposited. He expressed the idea that "many of the banks, especially in commercial cities, would gladly avail themselves of such a provision to withdraw their circulation and substitute gold notes, convertible on demand into coin." He sums up his argument by saying: "If we are sincere in wishing specie payments, we must not only multiply the demands for coin; we must encourage contracts, issue coin notes both by the United States and by the banks, and thus, without contraction, dispense with the use of the inferior and depreciated currency."

This is a plan of *gradual substitution of gold certificates* of large and small denominations, (the large by the Treasury, the small by the banks, it may be supposed,) for existing greenbacks and national bank notes.

These plans are based upon entirely different theories; that of Mr. McCulloch, for resumption by the Treasury under certain conditions, and that of immediate resumption by Mr. Greeley, assume that the *ratio of reserve to issue*—that is, of coin in the Treasury to greenbacks in circulation—is the true measure of safety; but on a closer view it seems that it is only a secondary measure. The true principle for the maintenance of an equality between coin and currency is to be found in the correct *ratio of coin in the country to the circulating medium* of the country—in other words, in the specie strength of the general circulation. The one may provide a proper basis for a resumption by the Treasury alone, though it is not probable it could be maintained, even with a much larger sum than the Treasury has ever yet held; the other establishes the ground for a general resumption.

The objection to these plans is, that by locking up coin in the Treasury they keep up the price of gold. If, on the contrary, the gold be let loose and added to the present circulating medium, without other action, that of itself will produce an inflation under which prices will again rise, the medium be again contracted through some sudden want of confidence, and gold again disappear. Never were truer words uttered than those of Mr. McCulloch, when he said: "It is a well-established fact that the demand for money increases (by reason of the advance of prices) with the supply, and that this demand is not unfrequently most pressing when the volume of currency is the largest and inflation has reached the culminating point." This applies to all purely paper and to all mixed currencies.

The plan of Mr. Sherman recognised the truth, that there must be substitution and not contraction, and he proposed, by what seems a most cumbrous plan, the gradual passage of the banks and Treasury into a new system. The great objections to it are that, during the long process, it would add to our existing currencies still another measure of values, and the certainty that no such round-about ways are now necessary if we are at specie point.

If gold is worth more than par, there is no possibility of resumption. When it reaches the par of greenbacks it will float in the currency, and by so much as it floats supply the demand for money and diminish the premium on greenbacks.

The true plan for resumption is this: The taking in of the greenbacks as gold flows into circulation, substituting coin for paper without contraction or change of values, arresting the process when money rises above seven per cent., resuming it as it becomes cheap, and thus gradually absorbing gold into our circulating medium. When we hold the same amount of coin in proportion to our paper currency that France or Great Britain always hold in proportion to their paper currencies, we may not only declare but maintain a legal resumption. Until then, in spite of all plans, the experience of nations tells us that this result cannot be reached. No nation has yet floated any large amount of paper and kept it on a par with gold, with even an equal amount of coin in its circulating medium.

In the plan proposed, the gradual substitution of coin for currency in our circulating medium, there need be no forced change of values. The country will itself resume and take and use the gold as it appears. It is only needful to guard against the inflation which even the entry of gold into that medium when it floats at par will cause, by an order of Congress requiring the Secretary of the Treasury to withdraw currency as coin appears.

That gold will be at par before the meeting of Congress there is little doubt. Indeed, it cannot be otherwise. The time for the withdrawal of the fractional currency has already arrived. Large sums of silver are already refused in exchange for greenbacks in this city.

If Gen. GRANT makes up his mind to recommend to Congress "to fight it out on this line"—the line of gradual resumption—there is ground for a reasonable hope that specie payment may be fully restored in his term of office.

He will not surely allow his practical mind to be swayed from its purpose by the loud cries of the inflationists. The traders who move the crops may cry for more currency; the farmers who make the crops, whose crops are moved, demand more value in the currency. The manufacturer may cry for expansion; the artisan, the workman, demand a better measure of value. The cry for inflation may be the cry of all those who live by the labor of others; the cry for specie is the cry of the people. They are weary of unsettled prices, and know full well, that often as the load of decline may be shifted, it is upon their shoulders that it must fall at last.

If the President holds firmly to this purpose, and the return to specie payment be the result of the financial policy of his administration, he will earn and receive the blessing of a grateful people, and add a leaf to the chaplet of his fame which will not pale even beside those which tell of the greatest victories of his triumphal career.

KNICKERBOCKER.

NEW-YORK, *October* 14, 1873.

Letter No. IX.

OUR GOLD RESOURCES.

THE fall in gold and the probability that the market must still further decline, under the large shipments which have but begun from England to this country, warrant the belief that par will be reached before Congress meets in its ordinary course. For the first time since the disappearance of the precious metals in 1861 it seems possible to begin to restore coin to its proper place in the circulating medium of the country.

The circulating medium does not now seem to be excessive. We have only to keep it at its present amount, allow values gradually to settle themselves to its measure and take steps to improve the medium itself. To improve the medium it is not necessary either to lessen or to add to it. It must neither be contracted nor expanded. It must be held firmly at the present point, and a gradual substitution of coin for currency be made. As fast as gold appears in circulation at par, a permanent place must be made for it in the circulating medium by a retirement of an equal amount of paper. The gauge of this transfer will be the price of money ; when it rises above seven per cent. in the financial centres the process must be stopped ; when it falls below this amount it may be always safely resumed without any change in values.

The chief element in this process of substitution of coin is the sum of specie now here, or which may be hoped for in the course of the coming year. It is, indeed, a strange anomaly that this country, the new Eldorado of the world, the great producer of the metals which the universal experience of mankind has chosen as the standard of value, should be the only country where these metals are disregarded and cried down as " relics of barbarism unworthy of our age." Yet so long as we make a part of the financial world, we must, in some form, accommodate ourselves to the standard of value in general use.

The Treasury Department reported the total amount of gold and silver of domestic production, deposited at the United States Mint and branches, for coinage, from the beginning of the Government to June 30, 1872:

Gold,	$836,205,463 50
Silver,	23,065,499 24
Total,	$859,270,962 74

Under ordinary circumstances the mode by which to arrive at an approximate idea of the amount of this product now remaining in the country, would be to deduct from it the total amount reported by the Treasury as exported up to same period. The remainder would stand for the sum of gold now in the country. This process would entirely disregard, on the one hand, the large amounts of coin taken out of the country by private individuals, travelers, &c., of which no exact account can be had; but, on the other hand, it would also disregard the equally large amount, though in smaller sums, brought into the country by immigrants. A still much larger amount should also be allowed in such estimate for that withdrawn from circulation and used in plate and in the general arts.

The general estimate of the amount of coin in circulation in 1860 was that of $250,000,000.

The Treasury Department reported the coinage of the mint to the 30th June:

	Gold.	Silver.	Total.
1861,	$80,708,400 64	$2,883,706 94	$83,592,107 58
1862,	61,676,576 55	3,231,081 51	64,907,658 06
1863,	22,645,729 90	1,564,297 22	24,210,027 12
1864,	23,982,748 31	850,086 99	24,882,835 30
1865,	30,685,699 95	950,218 69	31,635,918 64
Total,	$219,699,155 35	$9,479,391 35	$229,178,546 70

On the other hand, the Treasury Department reported the amount of exports and imports of gold and silver to 30th June:

	Exports.	Imports.
1861,	$29,791,080	$46,339,611
1862,	36,886,956	16,415,052
1863,	64,156,611	9,584,105
1864,	105,244,350	13,115,612
1865,	67,643,226	9,810,072
Total,	$303,722,223	$95,264,452

Showing an excess of exports over imports of $208,460,771 from 1860 to 1865. If we then take the estimated amount of coin in the country,

In 1860, say... $250,000,000
Add coinage from 1860 to 1865,....................... 229,178,546

Total,... $479,178,546
And deduct the excess of exports,.................... 208,460,771

There remains as amount of coin in 1805,.............. $270,717,775

Under ordinary conditions this would be a fair statement of the then existing amount of specie in the country. Unfortunately for any thing like even comparative nearness of estimate, there enters into it the disturbing element of war. How is it possible to estimate the amounts of coin which were hoarded in the South during the war? How much coin found its way to the South and passed out of the country through its ports and overland by Mexico?

Still, as the subject is examined, the conviction inevitably results that the amount of coin in private hands in the country is greatly under estimated.

Those who refuse to accept the deductions from positive premises, must show the falseness of the premises before they attack the conclusion which depends on them.

Resuming then the foregoing calculation, the sum of $270,000,000 is the starting point for the sum of specie in the country 30th of June, 1865.

We will now resume the Treasury tables since that date.
The coinage of the Mint was as follows :

	Gold.		Silver.		Total.
1866,..............	$37,429,430 46	..	$1,506,646 58	..	$39,026,077 04
1867,..............	39,838,878 82	..	1,562,694 18	..	41,401,573 00
1868,..............	24,141,235 06	..	1,592,986 48	..	25,734,221 54
1869,..............	32,027,966 03	..	1,574,037 17	..	33,602,903 20
1870,..............	30,103,364 75	..	2,670,054 16	..	32,773,418 91
1871,..............	34,403,504 42	..	5,500,085 38	..	39,903,649 80
1872,..............	36,193,187 73	..	13,421,779 37	..	49,614,967 10
Total,......	$234,137,627 27	..	$27,919,183 32	..	$262,056,810 59

The amount of exports and imports of gold and silver for the same period was:

	Exports.		Imports.
1866,	$86,044,071	....	$10,700,092
1867,	60,868,372	....	22,070,475
1868,	93,784,102	....	14,188,368
1869,	57,138,380	....	19,807,876
1870,	58,155,666	....	26,419,179
1871,	98,441,988	....	21,270,024
1872,	79,877,534	....	13,743,689
Total,	$534,310,113	....	$128,199,703

Showing an excess of exports over imports of $406,110,410.
If we then take the estimated amount of coin in the country:

In 1865, say	$270,000,000
Add coinage, 1865 to 1872,	262,056,810
Total,	$532,056,810
And deduct the excess of exports, 1865 to 1872,	406,110,410
There remains an amount of coin in 1872,	$125,946,400

Now, on the 30th June, 1872, the Treasury and banks held a sum exceeding one hundred millions. A careful review of this subject leads inevitably to the conclusion, that sufficient account has never been taken in this country of the sums of coin in private hoard.

In the preceding no consideration has been given to the sums of bullion which, passing through private assay, are not included in the tables of the Treasury Department.

What are the present coin resources independent of this apparent large private hoard, which, being a sum uncertain, indefinite, and not to be proven, must be left out of the calculation?

The report of the Treasury for the 1st October, 1873, stated the amount of coin in the Treasury at $80,246,757 54. The national banks held, at the last September showing, $18,844,600, of which, perhaps, (not represented by the Treasury in its gold certificates,) say $10,000,000. There is estimated to be in outside holding, say $40,000,000; total sum, say $130,000,000. There is on the way from Europe, or lately arrived, $10,000,000; allowing for further receipts from Europe of $10,000,000, we have in all a grand total of coin of $150,000,000, upon which it is safe to calculate before the 1st January, 1873.

Is this not a safe basis upon which to commence the substitution of coin for greenbacks?

For a legal resumption by the Treasury before that period, or at that period, certainly not; but with the certainty that we shall have this amount of coin, there seems to be no reason why a substitution of coin for greenbacks in the circulating medium may not be undertaken so soon as gold falls to par.

For the year 1874 we may safely rely on some addition to our coin from Europe, surely enough with our own productions to make up the sum of $50,000,000 more. Why may we not take a large part of this sum also into our circulating medium?

What need be feared? It is shown that in the years from 1866 to 1872 the Mint has received and coined two hundred and sixty millions of dollars; that in that same period we have been able to export four hundred millions of the precious metals. What need be feared?

So long as we were running on upon inflated values, to which no check had been given by an arrest of confidence in an exorbitant system of credit, based on a paper system, there was no chance of any plans of even gradual resumption by a substitution of coin for paper. But now that it has been found that there is a day of judgment and settlement for transactions in paper as well as for transactions in gold, it cannot be denied that if it be now possible to return to a gold basis the trial is worth making.

In the foregoing statements, based upon the latest figures of the Treasury Department, the history of this last year's transactions has been disregarded. It has already been shown that our shipments of coin have largely fallen off—to an extent since the 1st January up to the 1st October, 1873, as against those of 1872, of $17,000,000, and against 1873 of $28,000,000. Our imports had diminished in the same period $27,000,000. No one who has watched the movement of trade during the present month has failed to notice the enormous increase in our exports. They are already at this date $53,000,000 in excess of those of 1872, for same period. It is too early to take note of the decrease in imports. The effect of the panic had hardly been felt at the date of the last official statement; but it is not unsafe to say that fully one-half of the orders for imports of foreign goods have to-day been canceled. The importer would be wild indeed who, in the face of our recent stringency in money, shrinkage in prices, and uncertainty as to the future of the market here, would leave orders outstanding that could be canceled. While unfortunately, therefore, there still exists great difficulty in the movement of produce, and our crops may yet wait before reaching the hungry markets which await them, it is nevertheless sure that every bushel of wheat on which Europe depends for subsistence, and every bale of cotton which is necessary to enable her working men to earn the means of subsistence, will sooner or later be taken from us and paid for in coin. Only let us wisely seize the opportune moment to deny ourselves that which we may very well do without for a time at least, and while sending to Europe that which she must have for life's sake, restore that preponderance which the food-producing nations can always maintain over the food-purchasing nations in the trade of the world.

Only to this end let us no longer delude ourselves with the idea that paper is money, or exchangeable otherwise than as the representative of value. That representative of value, like all others, must be measured by the inevitable standard of value, so long as we find it necessary or profitable to trade with foreign nations.

It cannot be believed, that when our people look upon the vast resources of this country, its enormous product of the precious metals, that it will consent to part with them with such indifference. How strange the spectacle, that the country can witness an export of fifty or sixty millions a year of gold and silver with indifference, and yet hail with such joy as it has shown the return of ten millions. The measure of our prodigality is full. Let us now take pride in showing the world that a country, which in eight years has redeemed six hundred millions of its national debt, while exporting four hundred millions of coin, can now, without other effort than its own powers of production and economy, and by a simple and natural process, return to specie payment, and enter once more into the great family of financial nations.

Then we may indeed feel that we were not wrong in the judgment so often set forth during the great rebellion, that the supreme effort to maintain the unity of the country was not only in our physical power, but wholly within our money resources.

KNICKERBOCKER.

NEW-YORK, *October* 17, 1873.

Letter, No. X.

WHAT SHALL WE DO WITH IT?

SPECIE in coin and bullion is rapidly flowing in upon us, and there is no reason to believe that this natural course will be stopped for a long period. We may look for many millions more before there be even a lull in the movement. England has not yet bought any considerable part of the grain and cotton which are absolutely needful to her, and so long as she continues her purchases she must pay us in hard cash. So great is the want, and so large the competition for its supply, that even the steamers are called upon to the utmost of their freight capacity. Those of the English, French and German lines went out on Saturday heavily laden, and those for the present week have full cargoes engaged. The small demand for bills adds value to every moment that can be saved in getting the coin returns for this export.

The Bank of England has raised its rate of interest to seven per cent., but that is no proof of any unwillingness on her part to send coin to the United States, but only of her intention to keep up her own strength under the withdrawal of coin for shipment. The raising of the rate of interest serves the double purpose of checking trade and of attracting money to the bank vaults. Just so soon as the transfer of money from the other financial centres of Europe—Paris, Frankfort, Vienna, Amsterdam—becomes profitable, coin will flow from them to England, to take advantage of the advanced premium.

Were this not the case, the elasticity of the circulating medium of England itself would be fully equal to the strain upon it. It would be strange, indeed, if this wealthy nation, which has taken the greater part of the large sums of specie shipped by us during past years, cannot now spare us even a small percentage of that sum without general distress.

The returns of the Treasury Department published Saturday last, give the net amount of specie exported during the fiscal year ending June 30, 1873, as $63,127,637; bringing up the net outgo of specie since the close of the war, i. e., from July, 1866, to July, 1873, to $469,238,047.

So far from the Bank of England looking with regret upon the return of specie to this country, there is every reason to believe that the directors of this institution would be the first to hail with joy the resumption of specie payment by the United States. Much interested as the foreign bankers and gold brokers may be in the fluctuation of values which give them such chances of rapid and large profits, the great banks themselves know well that their true interest is in steady markets and even money rates.

Surely it cannot be for their interest that the United States should remain shut out from the family of specie-paying nations one day longer than can be avoided.

The *Saturday Review*, in its number of October 4, clearly hints at this feeling in saying : " The causes of the money difficulties are clearly understood in England, and it will be a matter for regret if the Government of the United States has resorted to any empirical attempt to relieve the pressure. But for the existence of an inconvertible paper currency, the arrival of gold from Europe would probably soon have enabled the banks to meet their liabilities."

The view taken by one of your neighbors of Printing-House Square in saying that the shipment of a few more millions of gold from England to the United States is " certain to be disastrous to both countries," is not a correct view, and the result will so prove.

There is little doubt that but for the unwise and persistent policy of the Treasury Department in upholding the gold market, specie would be now floating in the country on a par with greenbacks, and the much-talked of " redeemability and convertibility " be to-day a practical fact.

A simple comparison of the Treasury balances, at the beginning and at the close of the money panic, will show how far the policy of stopping sales and hoarding receipts has been carried. The Treasurer reported :

	Coin in Treasury.	Outstanding Certificates.	Belonging to United States.
20th September,...............	$83,623,595	$36,194,700	$47,428,895
11th October,..................	82,099,582	31,213,400	50,886,182
Decrease,..................	$1,524,013	$4,981,300	....
Increase,...................	....	....	$3,457,287

Showing that while holders of certificates withdrew coin to the amount of five millions, the Treasury increased the amount at its own disposal by the sum of three and a half millions in the same period.

From these figures it may be seen how much the policy of the Secretary has contributed to hold up the price of gold. No one with any knowledge of the gold market, or who has watched its course, believes that there was any such amount as five millions on the market until the arrivals from Europe. Yet, under the stoppage of the sales of the Treasury and a determined effort on the part of the gold brokers to force up the price, it rose from 112 to 115, to fall as rapidly to 108. The course is now downward, in spite of slight fluctuations depending on the bankers' movement from day to day. Meanwhile large amounts must soon come on the market; the assay office and mints are turning out the sums left with them for stamp and coinage ; there are at least ten millions more afloat on the way from Europe, and new shipments are daily announced. To add to this the Treasury itself must put out $13,500,000 on the 1st November in payment of interest, and some of the States pay out considerable sums, estimated in all to amount to $2,000,000. Here is a sum of *thirty to thirty-five millions* which will be afloat on the 1st of next month, not fifteen days distant.

Nor is this the end of the movement. There is much talk about the terrible effect abroad of our taking back a few crumbs of that rich store which we have been sending to Europe of late years, and threats of a return of Government bonds to turn the trade balance ; but as the threats do not come from those who hold Government bonds, they may be disregarded. There is no greater error than to treat the money capitalists of Europe as a unit, either in interest or in action. Just as with us there was small desire to sell Government securities during the panic, just so in Europe the holders of our bonds are, in the general, those who have no interest in ordinary trade. The bonds were bought and are held for investment. The rise and fall in price does not affect the holder so long as he be sure of his interest, and this he will not fail to be if we do not tamper with the Government credit, by breaking faith as to the collection of even a part of the Customs in other than coin.

The recent slight rise here in the price of gold of the early days of last week, was based on an idle rumor that one of the large foreign houses had sold one million of Government bonds. The truth was only half stated. The million of bonds were sold here, but the foreign branch of the house repurchased the same day abroad, and the bankers here were in funds to take a million of dollars of produce bills at the low rates then ruling.

There need be no fear of any return of Government securities from Europe, that is certain. The holders of rail-road securities are of a different order ; but there is little to tempt any sale of this class of securities in the present depressed state of the market.

There is, then, no doubt but that the sum of specie coming to us is very large. *What shall we do with it ?* It is clear enough what the people intend to do with it ; they intend to resume, and to pay it out just so far as it will go.

It only remains for Congress to provide for it a permanent resting-place in the circulating medium, and it will remain with us. If, on the contrary, currency is not withdrawn as gold appears, the gold itself, added to that circulating medium, will cause another inflation, expand bank discounts, provoke importation, turn the balance of trade against us, and again drive out coin from the country. When will our financiers see the truth which France has always recognised, that the true flexibility of a circulating medium should be in coin and not in paper; that it is a profound error to meet financial disaster with paper plasters; that when general distrust is produced by over-trading there is no way to avoid liquidation, and that it is more just and fair that the suffering and loss which is caused by that liquidation should fall by contraction on the shoulders of those to which it belongs, than by expansion be shifted to other and innocent shoulders?

The truth is, very little legislation is necessary. Let us have a respite for the present from any new plans of finance. If Congress will provide a place in the circulating medium for the coin we are sure to have at the time of its session, it need go no further. This place should be made in the first instance by the withdrawal of greenbacks. The Secretary should be ordered to take them in as fast as coin arrives to take their place, and the condition of the money market permits. Gold cannot again rise above par if the circulating medium be kept at its present point—seven hundred millions—the sum now generally allowed to be not in excess of the needs of the country. The dearness of money would keep it in circulation, and the price of money be the gauge by which the Secretary could measure the time and amount of withdrawal.

The balance of trade would not be turned against us, because the banks, forced to prepare themselves for the day when the Treasury itself would resume, would so stop discounts as to check imports. It is a source of regret that this withdrawal of currency should not be of the national bank notes; but a moment's reflection will show how cumbrous such a withdrawal would be, and how impossible to distribute the gradual reduction equally among the banks. There is no doubt that the people have lost their confidence in the national bank issues and prefer the greenbacks. Yet it would be unjust, after the recent suffering of the banks, to inflict on them the further loss which such a measure would involve.

It will be a simple measure when a large part of the greenback issue has been taken in, and the remainder made convertible into coin at the Sub-Treasuries, to call in the whole bank circulation, and pay off the United States bonds on which it is based by a new issue of the convertible greenbacks.

It is needless here to notice the effect that such a withdrawal of bonds would have upon our national credit. There would be a saving of fifteen to twenty millions a year in interest, and the debt itself would be not much in excess of fifteen hundred millions—a sum which would be held beyond the contingencies of money markets, and eagerly sought for permanent holding both at home and abroad. Our circulating medium, consisting of seven hundred millions, half greenbacks and half coin, would unite the best qualities of the famed systems of France and England—an amount of coin, as in France, as large or larger than the issue of paper—an issue of paper, as in England, so limited that it cannot fall below the par of coin ; in addition, the American principle of a reserve in coin in the Treasury equal to twenty or twenty-five per cent. of the greenback issue.

The product of coin in the country would yearly supply quite as much additional circulating medium as the country would require, and render it yearly better and stronger. We have contributed since the beginning of the Government more than nine hundred millions of specie to the store of the world. We have drained ourselves of it much further than it was safe to do. Now that, in the order of nature, we have for the first time a chance to control its course, let us not hesitate to grasp it. Let us henceforth keep our own precious metals, at least our full share of them. Now is our hour. Neglect it and to-morrow it may be too late. Can there be a doubt as to what our choice will be as to the specie—as to *what we shall do with it ?* The country will soon ask that question, and its answer will be, *We shall keep it.*

KNICKERBOCKER.

NEW-YORK, *October* 20, 1873.

Letter No. XI.

FLEXIBILITY IN THE CURRENCY.

IMMEDIATELY upon the opening of Congress there will be laid before it several schemes of finance, each proposing to remedy present distress and to provide against like disasters in the future.

Of these the best known are that of Mr. Senator SHERMAN, proposed in July, 1868, and January, 1869, for the issue of convertible notes by the United States Treasury to banks upon the deposit of Government bonds, and that for a new Bank Law, brought forward by Mr. FREEMAN CLARKE, late Comptroller of the Currency, in January, 1872.

The main features of each of these is to provide flexibility in the currency. The need of some sort of flexibility has been clearly shown in the late crisis, the circulating medium being limited by law to a fixed sum. When, from distrust or other causes, this fixed sum proved insufficient, there was no relief—the viciousness of our system of paper money being an absolute bar to any aid from other nations, or to any relief from the money store of the world—otherwise the gold arriving would have already provided relief. It must not be supposed that the gold now flowing in upon us comes to us because of the distress in our money market. It is not to us a part of the floating capital of the world, seeking employment where it is to be had to best advantage, but a mere commodity sent here to be bartered for such other commodities, grain and cotton, as we have in abundance and other nations greatly need. Had there been no crisis, the flow of gold would have taken place, though, perhaps, it would not have lasted so long as is now probable.

There is, it is true, a sum of forty-four millions in the Treasury of the United States, the remainder of the sum by which Mr. Secretary McCulloch contracted the legal tender issues under the act of April, 1866, and which has been again, as during the summer of that memorable year 1867, the bone of financial contention. The importance of the controversy, except as it regards the interpretation of the law, has been greatly overrated. The issue of this sum of forty-four millions would afford no such relief as has been claimed for it. It would have been, after all, but an addition of six per cent. to the circulating medium of the country, which now exceeds seven hundred millions. A considerable part is needed by the banks to bring up their reserves to the legal point. It must not be forgotten that this reserved currency is of the legal tender issue, and therefore would have been taken up and hoarded in the same way as the rest of that circulation has been. The withdrawal in currency not being of the bank note issues, but of the greenback issues, to which legislation has given exceptional value, this reserve would add but little flexibility, even if issued, and when once issued would never return to its original place as reserve, but be absorbed in the medium which it would itself have inflated. Only a direct contraction would restore it to the Government for similar use in similar emergency, and we know what Congress thinks of contraction. As Mr. Boutwell naively remarked in his address of Tuesday evening, "It is much easier for a Government to extend the volume of currency than it is to reduce it." Yet to issue that reserve to-day, when the market is recovering from the pressure, would be to inflate values and retard the near approach of specie resumption. The theory of Mr. Secretary RICHARDSON is the true one. If the forty-four millions be used at all, it must be for Government purposes, and to provide for unforeseen contingencies in Government finances. And this should be settled, beyond a doubt, as early as possible by an order of Congress.

To return to the plan proposed by Mr. SHERMAN. In his speech in the Senate, Jan. 27, 1869, he laid down as the requisites of a good currency :

" 1. That it be a paper currency. 2. That it be amply secured, either by the credit of a nation or by unquestioned collaterals. 3. That, except in extreme cases of panic, it be convertible into coin. 4. That provision be made for a suspension of the right to demand coin during such panics."

The objections to this plan are obvious. What is a panic? When does it begin and when does it end? If the crisis of 17th to 20th September had closed on the latter day, (Saturday,) would it or would it not have constituted a panic within Mr. SHERMAN's meaning? Probably not. Yet had the relief by the issue of currency in purchase of bonds by the Treasury been given on Friday, instead of Saturday, the stoppage of the Union Trust Company would have been, perhaps, avoided, and the panic have ceased, or, at least, its violence have been checked. Liquidation would, however, have gone on; when once begun, it seldom stops before it is thoroughly ended. The public like, now and then, to take soundings even in the wildest expansions, and when they begin they do not stop sounding until they touch the bottom.

But the difficulty is not only to determine what a panic is, but *when* it exists. Who is to have this enormous power conferred upon him? Surely, the Secretary of the Treasury is not to be sole judge of such a grave matter, and if not he, who then? The banks cannot be allowed a part in such judgment, for then the disease might become chronic, and a state of panic become their normal condition. These are fatal objections. Mr. SHERMAN's plan of an interchangeability of notes and Government bonds would not provide such flexibility as is desired; he himself proposed a maximum to such issue and thus put a limit to its flexibility. Desirable as some features of his further plan of an issue of small gold notes may have appeared in 1869, when the approach to a specie level seemed so long and so beset with danger, they cannot now be so regarded, when, under judicious management and by simple process, general resumption may be gradually attained without their adoption.

The second plan, that of Mr. FREEMAN CLARKE, for a new banking law, allows to any bank the issue of as much circulation as it may choose to put out upon proper security; provides for a general agency where such notes shall be redeemed in legal tenders, and finally requires that the Government shall hold a reserve of 100 millions in coin for the redemption of its own notes.

This plan has greater flexibility than that of Mr. SHERMAN, but is all the more dangerous on that account. And it would be found in practice that the notes would be all travelling toward the agency for redemption just when they would be most wanted. Such was the case in 1857, when the action of the interior banks forced the suspension of the city banks after all need for such suspension had already passed. Nor does this scheme provide for any increase in the amount of coin in the country, and there is no safety in any plan which is not based on the *ratio of coin in the country to the amount of the circulating medium.* If there be no use provided for coin, it will not remain with us, but follow the same course it has taken of late years. The country will be in a continual state of paper inflation, and at another time of distrust, the issues of the banks certainly, and perhaps those of the Government, will be discredited. The present system is quite as good as this; and if to-day the Treasury held one hundred millions of coin and redeemed its issues, would work quite as well—at least until the exchanges again turned against us, when it is certain that with the limited supply of coin in use, it would find itself compelled to close its doors. The Treasury of the United States has no power of expansion or contraction. It cannot raise the price of money and attract it to its vaults, as the Bank of England does in times of pressure. Yet it would have to maintain at par an issue of 350 millions of dollars, (or 400 millions, if the reserve can be legally used,) on a coin basis of 100 millions. The Bank of England, on the 24th September, before the pressure for money had begun, held £21,632,321 in coin and bullion to an active note circulation of £26,678,140, or, say, of 110 millions dollars coin to 135 millions circulation; and this with the great money marts of Europe at her very door. Yet it is proposed that our treasury with the same reserve shall float three times the amount of paper that the Bank of England keeps out when her issues are the largest.

The position of France may be referred to, but gives no ground for comparison. There is only one paper circulation in France

—that of the Bank of France—and since the war its notes have not been convertible into coin. Yet in spite of her disasters, the whole issue of notes did not exceed, on the 2d of October, 2,947,323 francs, equal to, say, 590 millions dollars, while it held in cash and ingots the sum of 717,338,720 francs, or, say, 140 millions dollars. Gold is still at a premium great enough to keep it from general circulation, and will so continue until some withdrawal of paper issues be made. Even the Bank of France, though no longer paying coin, has, by raising the rate of discount, the power to sustain its position and attract money to its treasury.

In these systems all the *flexibility* is in the coin part of the circulating medium. The banks strengthen themselves by attracting money. In the FREEMAN CLARKE bill the unfortunate Treasury would be called upon, with a reserve of 100 millions of coin, to sustain directly an issue of 350 to 400 millions of paper, and indirectly of just as much more as the banks would find the country willing to take up. Here the flexibility is all on the wrong side.

There is still another plan proposed, that of a *general free banking law*, under which any individual may lodge bonds with the Treasury, and receive currency, or return the bonds and get back the currency at will. As the Government debt is gradually reduced, it would probably be found that the holders of bonds would not be those who would care to make such exchanges, and the scheme would practically defeat itself. This impracticability renders any further discussion of this scheme unnecessary.

If it were otherwise, there seems to be no reason why the Treasury Department should be turned into such a national pawnbroker's shop as this would make of it—where any one who wanted to take advantage of a fall in stocks could borrow money from and pledge his bonds with the United States Treasury.

Experience has certainly already shown us that United States bonds are the last things which are parted with in times of pressure. There is then no flexibility to be looked for here. *Where, then, is true flexibility to be found?* Only in the introduction of a large amount of coin into the circulating medium, by the substitution of coin for currency when gold shall be at par. This policy should be pursued until the amounts of gold and paper in circulation are about equal —say 350 millions coin and 350 millions paper. This can be reached most easily by withdrawing the greenbacks first. Later, a convertible issue of greenbacks may purchase the bonds on which the national notes are based, and replace them on their cancellation.

All restrictions on banking should be removed. The usury laws of the several States should be repealed by Congress. If it have not the clear authority under the Constitution, it should seek it by an amendment. Seven per cent. should be fixed as the legal rate where no contracts are made. The banks can be then confined to their legitimate business of deposit and discount, and, relieved from Government interference, transact their business each in its own way. The strong banks need no longer be forced to cast in their lot with the weak in time of trouble, and this premium upon imprudence be set aside. This would be true free banking.

The currency will thus be independent of the banks, and no combination of circumstances, accidental or designed, can keep it from the people to whom it belongs—while the product of our own soil will add as much coin each year to the circulating medium as the increasing business of the country may require. This, and the exemption of money from the usury restriction, which is, indeed, a "relic of barbarism," will give to the circulating medium the *flexibility* which it needs.

KNICKERBOCKER.

NEW-YORK, *October* 25, 1873.

Letter No. XII.

NOW OR NEVER.

THE DUTY OF THE GOVERNMENT AS REGARDS RESUMPTION.

As the hour approaches when, by the law of supply and demand, the premium upon gold must inevitably fall and finally wholly disappear, the power of the country to begin a gradual resumption by the absorption of specie into the circulating medium, is the main and paramount question. That gold will fall to par before the meeting of Congress, hardly admits of a doubt. During the month of October, the mints received for coinage the sum of ten millions of dollars. There are now about ten millions more on the way from Europe. The Treasury Department must pay out on the 1st November the sum of nearly fifteen millions in coin for interest, and on the 16th, fifteen millions for the loan of 1862 already called in; in all, a sum of fifty millions will be by the middle of next month upon the market. The same causes which have drawn to this side of the Atlantic the sum of twenty millions still continue, and show no sign of early stoppage. The supply, therefore, bids fair to be largely increased, while, on the other hand, there is no reason to look for any demand which can take up such a sum as fifty millions in this space of time. The bankers have their hands full in the movement of produce and cotton, and money will surely remain stringent enough to check any considerable speculation in gold, if such a spirit were likely under the prospect of an increasing supply. The circulating medium does not seem excessive. All the currency, both of greenback and national bank issues, is fully employed in the crop movement. Money will be in full demand. Now, then, is the moment to prepare to retire a part of the paper issues, as gold appears in circulation, and to make a permanent place for it in our daily uses. Not only does the present seem to be the favorable moment for the beginning of this substitution, but there are grave reasons to believe that if this chance be neglected it may not return to us for a long period of years.

A view of the amount of gold coin outstanding in the circulating mediums of Europe and America, is here of interest.

In the supplemental report on international coinage, made to the Department of State on the 8th April, 1870, by Mr. Samuel B. Ruggles, whose authority on this and kindred subjects is beyond question, the following table is given of the amounts of coin in the currencies of Europe and America at that date:

GOLD COIN OUTSTANDING.

I. In France, Belgium, Switzerland, and Pontifical States, ... $1,250,000,000
II. In Austria, Spain, Sweden, Greece and Roumania, ... 200,000,000
III. In Germany, (North and South,) Netherlands, Denmark, Norway, Portugal, Russia and Turkey, ... 300,000,000
IV. In the United Kingdom of Great Britain, ... 450,000,000
V. In the United States of America, ... 200,000,000
VI. In Canada, Mexico, Central and South America, ... 150,000,000

Total, ... $2,550,000,000

There have been some notable changes in this distribution since the date of this report. From one hundred to two hundred millions have passed from France to Germany in payment of the tribute of war, and the United States have lost at least fifty millions of the amount held by it in 1870, as a reference to the tables of production and export of specie will show.

In the seventeen years ending the 30th June, 1870, the United States had exported over $650,000,000 of gold coin and bullion beyond the amount imported, and thus provided for one-quarter of the vast sum of European and American coinage.

The amount of coin in circulation in the United States has been variously estimated at different periods. Mr. JAMES GUTHRIE, Secretary of the Treasury, in his report of 1854, gave the following estimates:

1852, gold and silver,.....:............................$204,000,000
1853, gold and silver,.................................. 236,000,000
1854, gold and silver,.................................. 241,000,000

In the year 1855 there began a great outflow of the precious metals from the United States. Silver had so risen in value from the Asiatic demand, that the French Government had undertaken to replace the coinage of France, which had been chiefly of silver, with gold. The constant and increasing supplies from California rendered this a favorable moment, and under the process, the balance of trade being against this country, a heavy exportation of coin to Europe commenced, which continued without stop until the Fall of 1860.

The following tables show this movement:

Exports and Imports of Gold and Silver, as by the reports of the Treasury Department, to June 30.

	Exports.		Imports.
1855,................................	$59,239,348	....	$3,659,812
1856,................................	45,745,485	....	4,207,632
1857,................................	69,136,922	....	12,461,799
1858,................................	52,703,147	....	19,274,496
1859,................................	63,887,321	....	7,434,789
1860,................................	66,546,239	....	8,550,135
Total,...................	$357,258,462	....	$55,588,663

—showing an excess of exports over imports of $301,669,799.

On the other hand, the amount of production is shown to have been:

Statement of Gold and Silver of domestic production deposited at the Mint to June 30.

	Gold.		Silver.		Total.
1855,....	$63,574,032 54	....	$371,336 85	....	$63,945,369 39
1856,....	59,608,609 50	....	294,472 55	....	59,903,082 05
1857,....	23,270,030 74	....	127,256 12	....	23,397,286 86
1858,....:	40,977,168 55	....	316,472 36	....	41,293,640 91
1859,....	27,213,557 15	....	273,167 47	....	27,486,724 62
1860,....	18,971,041 75	....	293,797 05	....	19,264,838 80
Total,..	$233,614,440 23		$1,676,502 40		$235,290,942 63

Comparing these amounts, we then find :

Excess of exports,...................................$301,669,799
Domestic product,................................... 235,290,942
                                                     _____
Loss of coin 1855—1860,....................... $66,378,857

The export movement continued during the Summer of 1860, until the total amount of loss nearly reached one hundred millions of dollars. This heavy drain ceased in October, and soon after the tide turned, and an inflow began to the United States which, with the amount of domestic product, increased the amount in the country by about ninety millions in the year 1860 to 1861. This favorable movement in its turn ceased toward the close of the year.

There were, again, many wide differences of opinion as to the amount of specie held by the country in the year 1860. In his report of 1861, Mr. JAMES POLLOCK, the Director of the Mint at Philadelphia, used these words : "From the most reliable data attainable, I estimate the amount of specie in the United States at this date, October, 1861, at from 275 to 300 millions of dollars." If we deduct from this amount the increase of the preceding year, which he himself says "has added about ninety millions to our stock of coin," we arrive at his estimate for 1860 of two hundred and ten millions as the amount of specie in the country.

Mr. Secretary McCulloch did not rate the amount so high in his report of 1867. He said : "The actual legitimate business of the country is not larger than it was in 1860, when three hundred millions of coin and bank notes was an ample circulating medium." As the bank notes in issue that year reached the sum of two hundred millions, there is room in his estimate for only one hundred millions as the stock of specie in the country.

Senator MORTON, of Indiana, in a speech on the finances in December, 1868, in the Senate, estimated the circulating medium in 1860 "at four hundred and fifty millions, of which the entire bank circulation was two hundred and two millions; in vaults of banks, eighty-eight millions of coin, and in the country, outside of banks, one hundred and fifty millions." His estimate of the specie was then for the year 1860, two hundred and forty millions.

Here, then, we have three estimates for this period : 1st. That of Mr. Secretary McCulloch, of one hundred millions; 2d. That of Mr. Pollock, Mint Director, of two hundred and ten millions; 3d. Of Mr. Senator Morton, of two hundred and forty millions.

When the amounts of exports, of imports, and of production of gold and silver come to be looked into, it will be found that the enormous exports of specie, from 1861 to 1873, can in no other way be accounted for, except by adopting a starting sum even larger than the estimate of Mr. Senator MORTON—and it will be admitted that two hundred and fifty millions is an inside figure. In this calculation the mode of estimate will be that taken by Mr. POLLOCK, viz.: the amount of deposits at the mint of coin and bullion of domestic production, adding thereto the foreign imports and deducting the exports.

The Treasury Department reported the amount of deposits of coin and bullion at the various mints, less the re-deposits, to the 30th of June, in the following sums:

	Gold.	Silver.	Total.
1861,	$69,084,523 74	$3,062,047 47	$72,146,571 21
1862,	42,945,659 23	2,477,571 78	45,423,231 01
1863,	22,153,244 55	1,548,592 76	23,701,837 31
1864,	23,078,922 94	933,818 55	24,012,741 49
1865,	26,979,793 76	1,003,055 33	27,982,849 09
1866,	30,188,202 53	1,723,516 71	31,911,719 24
1867,	32,968,338 20	1,568,710 19	34,537,048 39
1868,	23,117,766 44	1,473,559 40	24,591,325 84
1869,	31,178,779 34	1,761,478 66	32,940,258 00
1870,	27,931,390 99	2,477,397 11	30,408,788 10
1871,	34,339,784 23	4,797,619 90	39,137,404 13
1872,	37,811,623 60	8,605,830 24	46,417,453 84
Total,	$401,778,029 55	$31,433,198 10	$433,211,227 65

On the other hand, the Treasury Department reported the amount of exports and imports of gold and silver for same period to 30th June:

	Exports.	Imports.
1861,	$29,791,080	$46,339,611
1862,	36,886,956	16,415,052
1863,	64,156,611	9,584,105
1864,	105,244,350	13,115,612
1865,	67,646,226	9,810,072
1866,	86,044,071	10,700,092
1867,	60,869,372	22,070,475
1868,	93,784,102	14,188,368
1869,	57,138,380	19,807,876
1870,	58,155,666	26,419,179
1871,	98,441,988	21,270,024
1872,	79,877,534	13,743,689
Total,	$838,035,836	$223,464,155

Returning now to the estimate named, of the amount of—

Coin in 1860,..	$250,000,000
Adding deposits in mint, 1860 to 1872..................	433,211,227
And imports of foreign coin, 1860 to 1872,..............	223,464,155
Total,.......................	$906,675,382
And deducting exports of coin and bullion, 1860 to 1872,..	838,035,336
There remained as coin, June 30, 1872,..........	$68,640,046

Now, as it is known that the amount in the Treasury and banks at that date exceed one hundred millions, it is clear either that the starting point of 250 millions was too low an estimate of the coin in the country in 1860, or else that the amount of bullion assayed by private individuals—which being taken note of by the Custom House, appears in the export column, while as it did not pass through the mint, it does not appear in the column of domestic production—was sufficient to account for this large difference. The writer published a calculation in his communication of the 17th of October, based upon the tables of the coinage of the country. To this it has been objected that it did not make proper allowance for the amount of imported specie, which, passing through the mint for coinage, thus appeared twice in the estimate. Starting at the point of 250 millions in 1860, the sum of 126 millions was reached as that remaining in the country June 30, 1872. The results of both of these calculations are below any reasonable estimate.

If we take as the probable stock June 30, 1872,...................	$150,000,000
Add estimate of product for 1872–73,...........................	35,000,000
And imports to June 30, 1873,.................................	21,480,937
Total,..	$206,480,937
And deduct exports to June 30, 1873,.........................	84,608,574
There remained in stock June 30, 1873,.......................	$121,872,363

A sum we again find too small, for on that day the Treasury held eighty-eight millions, and the banks of New-York alone, by their statement of June 28, 1873, twenty-four millions, in all, a sum of one hundred and twelve millions, without any account of the amount on the street or in private hands or held by other banks.

Another estimate then becomes necessary. The following may be safely taken as the minimum of the stock to-day:

In Treasury, October 1,	$80,246,757
In New-York banks, September 9, as by statement,	14,585,810
In outside holding,	40,000,000
Total,	$134,832,567
Received in October,	10,000,000
Total,	$144,832,567

This is coinage enough to begin the process of substitution with, if by the fall of gold to par it be clearly shown that the circulating medium is not in excess. A few weeks will settle this point. If we are not now to make the effort, what probability is there that we shall ever attempt to resume?

A reference to the foregoing tables shows, that while from 1861 to 1872 the excess of exports over imports of the precious metals reached the sum of $614,571,181, the production in same period only amounted to $433,211,227. So that we lost not only all of the product of our mines, but $181,359,954 from our stock. If we add to this the difference between excess of exports of sixty-three millions for the year ending June 30, 1873, over the production of same period, estimated at thirty-five millions—say a loss of thirty millions—the sum total of our loss is carried to the enormous figure of over two hundred and ten millions. Nor need we console ourselves with the thought that we could not help ourselves—that the war was the cause of this great loss—for, on closer examination, we shall find that from the 30th July, 1860, to the 30th July, 1865, this loss was only $15,193,541, while from 1865 to 1872 it amounted to $166,166,413; and if our product did not last year exceed that of 1871–72, the loss in the single year 1872–73 will exceed that of the whole war period. Can we quietly sit still and see this draining of our life-blood at such terrible rate? It is not possible. If we do, and our production of the precious metals remain the same as at present, and we continue to lose coin at the rate of the last decade, we shall arrive at the centennial of our independence with the disgraceful record, that since we became a nation we shall have produced and coined to the value of ONE THOUSAND MILLIONS DOLLARS of gold and silver, while the unfortunate Secretary of the Treasury may hardly know whither to turn for a sufficient sum to pay the interest on the Government debt. When that day comes, the difference will be found out between coin and paper, and the country will learn to its cost that no law will avail to check the rate the European money holder will exact for that which we now let slip from us, with a prodigality for which no equal can be found in the history of the world. A genera- ·

tion is rapidly coming forward that has never seen or handled the national coin which we yet have been stamping with a dissolving image by the hundred millions. If we hesitate now or falter, our children may go to their graves as ignorant as they have been from their cradle. It is indeed *now or never* that this wild folly must be stopped. But we will not hesitate. So soon as the people take note of these stern facts, there will be a movement which will rock the country like an earthquake; an upheaval of the popular conscience which will unhinge party machinery, tear asunder political ties, and threaten the very life of the great organization which now controls the destinies of the Republic.

The country looks trustfully to the President in this crisis. With his strong common sense, he will sooner or later find the sure road and lead the country in safety, through the perils which threaten it, to the repose for which it yearns.

He has already entered on the true path in the order to withdraw the fractional currency and replace it with silver. In this trial measure he will find that silver will float in the currency in the precise rate in which paper is withdrawn. As there is an abundance of fractional currency the two cannot float together—one must be withdrawn in part to make room for the other. From the result of this trial the true manner of restoring gold to the currency may be established. There can be no doubt as to what the result will be. By substitution, only, without increasing the circulating medium, can the passage from a paper to a gold basis be effected.

Let the President take the lead in this, the greatest measure of his administration. Let him remember the pilgrim's parable. Toward the close of Christian's progress it is related "That it was Little Faith that fell into the hands of the rogue Mistrust, and lost the most of his spending money, though he had a little odd money left, but scarce enough to bring him to his journey's end, so that he went with a hungry belly the most part of the rest of the way." It was Hopeful who, taking Christian by the hand, led him through the dangerous slumbers of the Enchanted Ground to the beautiful land of Beulah.

So may the President, with good courage and self-reliant strength, lead the country through the dangers which beset it, to boundless and sure prosperity.

KNICKERBOCKER.

NEW-YORK, *October* 29th, 1873.

www.ingramcontent.com/pod-product-compliance
Lightning Source LLC
Chambersburg PA
CBHW031753090426
42739CB00008B/993